PRACTICING PSYCHOTHERAPY

PRACTICING PSYCHOTHERAPY
Basic Techniques and Practical Issues

Edmund C. Neuhaus, Ph.D.
The Rehabilitation Institute
Mineola, New York

William Astwood, Ph.D.
The Divorce Crisis Service
Brooklyn, New York

HUMAN SCIENCES PRESS
72 Fifth Avenue   3 Henrietta Street
NEW YORK, NY 10011   ● LONDON, WC2E 8LU

Printed in the United States of America
0123456789   987654321

Library of Congress Cataloging in Publication Data

Neuhaus, Edmund C
   Practicing psychotherapy, basic techniques and practical issues.

   Includes index.
   1. Psychotherapy. I. Astwood, William, joint author. II. Title.
RC480.N38   616.89'14   LC 79-25464
ISBN 0-87705-467-3

Dedicated to our parents, teachers, and patients
who taught us so much

CONTENTS

ACKNOWLEDGMENTS

The authors wish to express their thanks and appreciation to several individuals for their invaluable help during the preparation of this manuscript.

Mrs. Anne Johnston provided untiring secretarial and editorial assistance. Her excellent sense of language contributed immeasurably in helping us minimize professional jargon and maintain a clear and straightforward presentation.

A much admired and esteemed colleague, Louise Friedman, was a continual source of practical advice that aided us in developing and clarifying our ideas.

Special gratitude goes to Olga Neuhaus and Sharon Sprung Astwood for their encouragement, patience, and understanding. Their emotional support was greatly needed and often severely tested when the authors' anxieties and struggles to complete this first book became too much to bear. Also, many thanks to Olga for the final typing, proofreading, and the myriad details necessary to bring this book to completion.

We have within us the power of seeing the things not seen and of making them visible. The truths that are most important to us are proved to be true not by reasoning about them or explaining them, but by acting upon them.

Our problem, the universal problem each one upon the earth must solve, is how to live.

Edith Hamilton
Witness To The Truth

INTRODUCTION

There is something intimidating about the idea of writing a book on psychotherapy, especially when the book is to be a guide for new therapists and, hopefully, a checkpoint for experienced therapists. There have been many times during a therapy session when the authors have been less than sure of what to do themselves. How then could we presume to tell others what they should do? This itself is the nature of the discipline. Not only must we be able to tolerate the ambiguity of our own situation, but we must also be able to share whatever knowledge we have with our patients and colleagues.

This book grew out of a growing realization that there is a dearth of information and discussion in textbooks and training situations concerning the practical issues and problems that occur daily in the practice of psychotherapy. During the many years of having been supervised and providing supervision to psychotherapists, the authors have been constantly confronted with questions that reflect a great unmet need: 1) to understand more about these everyday practical concerns and techniques of psychotherapy, and 2) how to deal effectively with them. Among these basic issues are the role of the patient and therapist in establishing therapeutic goals, beginning therapy, developing the therapeutic relationship, terminating therapy, and similar concerns that reflect the management of psychotherapy. Understandably, the answers to these questions come with time, training, and experience. But why wait for these answers? And so this book is directed primarily to the emerging or beginning psychotherapist from the disciplines of psychology, psychiatry, and social work who is looking for guidelines and an orientation that address themselves to these fundamental and recurring practical issues of psychotherapeutic practice. For the experienced therapist, perhaps this book will provide an opportunity to reevaluate basic concepts and techniques, and prove valuable in suggesting new ideas. We also believe that many of the concepts and techniques discussed can be of value to any profession (e.g., clergy, education) that counsels troubled and confused individuals.

Although the authors have been trained in and subscribe to a psychoanalytical philosophical framework, the ideas presented are not rooted in a specific theoretical school of psychotherapy. In no way is this book intended as a theoretical work that aims to deal with the infinite variety of issues that arises in a psychotherapeutic relationship. The goals of this book are modest: to provide an orientation for the novice clinician and a refresher for the experienced therapist regarding the daily concerns and basic techniques of psychotherapy. Although the techniques and ideas offered represent what the authors have found to be most effective as a result of their combined 30 years of therapeutic experience, we realize that our suggestions are not definitive, but a stimulus to growth as a psychotherapist. We hope that this book will be as helpful in the reading as it has been to us in the writing.

Chapter 1

A VIEW OF PSYCHOTHERAPY

DEFINITION

Psychotherapy is a concept that unfortunately tends to have as many definitions as there are authors writing on the subject. Despite the many definitions that are offered, psychotherapy can best be understood in terms of its basic technique and goal. Psychotherapy is viewed by the authors as a psychological technique aimed at alleviating the mental suffering of the patient and helping him or her develop more effective ways of coping with conflict or stress. Its ultimate goal is to develop greater personal integration, self-fulfillment, and broadened responsibility.

This definition recognizes that psychotherapy is essentially a psychological rather than a physical method. It relies primarily on verbal means of intervention and could be understood as a "talking cure." The importance of verbal communication implies a close interpersonal relationship between the client and therapist. The focus on learning to overcome symptoms and to deal more adequately with problems suggests that psychotherapy will impart a better degree of insight or understanding of oneself. However, we are aware that insight is not always necessary for psychotherapeutic success. Some individuals can achieve greater mental health and happiness by learning to react in different ways without recourse to acquiring "insight," or a deep understanding of the reasons for their behavior. Finally, this view of psychotherapy sees the individual as a suffering human being plagued with torment and anguish that requires compassion and, ultimately, healing.

THE SCIENCE VS. THE ART OF PSYCHOTHERAPY

Since the dawn of human experience there have been practitioners and methods of treating unusual or deviant behavior in human beings. The earliest known methods involved the mystical and magical rites of the shamans or medicine men and priests of primitive cultures. Usually the primary agent of healing was the effect of the actions and personality of the shaman upon the person seeking help. The effectiveness of the therapeutic medium rested on the quality of belief in the personal supernatural powers of the shaman-therapists. Although language and concepts differ in modern times, many of these psychodynamic principles still function in similar and/or identical ways. In a society as steeped in and dependent upon the scientific and technological method as our own, there tends to be an abiding discomfort with the psychotherapist. This discomfort is often expressed in vernacular expressions, which derive from these earlier times such as "headshrinker," "shrink," "witch doctor," or the 19th century term, "alienist." This connection of psychotherapy with the primitive and supernatural is still pervasive, especially in humor, which often reveals much about underlying attitudes in the general public. As an example, we are reminded of the cartoon depicting a patient leaving her therapist's office with the comment: "Oh doctor, I want to thank you.

You've opened my eyes to a whole new world of mumbo-jumbo."

The overwhelming success and influence of the scientific method over the past century has been especially noticeable in medicine. As a consequence, there has been an erosion of the authority of the traditional nonmedical specialties such as the clergy who dealt with people and their problems in living. Therefore, emotional distress and mental "illness" came more and more under the purview of the medical establishment. The "doctor" became the primary social agent charged with alleviating all abnormal or unusual human conditions. To their credit, physicians took on this burden and the scientific method led to great strides in physical medicine. Psychiatry and the treatment of emotional dysfunction, especially psychosis, however, have been more reluctant in yielding its secrets to scientific inquiry. Following the lead of physical medicine, clinicians and theorists initially sought an organic cause of mental disorders, hypothesizing that they were the result of brain lesions. These hypotheses eventually foundered on a lack of empirical evidence. Subsequently, the "organic" viewpoint gave way to the "psychological period," of which Sigmund Freud was one of the leading figures. Rigorously trained in the scientific method, Freud was the first to combine the philosophical and literary speculations about the human condition with the scientific method. In a sense, he combined the artistic tradition with the new scientific method and bridged what had been an apparent gap between the two. Basically, Freud brought the human individual into the medical study of behavior. He illustrated that what was occurring was not an impersonal disease process, but the interaction of the individual with his environment that produced the disorder. In doing so, Freud added the new-found powers of scientific investigation to those of the traditional philosophical and artistic speculations on human existence, rather than placing their individual truths to battle with and detract from each other.

Psychotherapy, as a professional discipline, is still in its scientific infancy. The methods of science have added to the understanding of human beings. They are not yet at the point, however, where they can completely substitute for the hard won, if somewhat ineffable, learning that proceeds from clinical experience and the intuitiveness of the therapist. The psychotherapist must daily confront the dilemma of being forced to cope with serious problems without a completely adequate body of theory and technique for assistance. In these existential moments, decisions must be made. In these moments, the controversy between science and art becomes irrelevant.

From this admittedly oversimplified, but pertinent, historical overview we can see how the question of whether psychotherapy is a science or art originated and developed. Attempting to arrive at an answer usually leads to a futile exercise in philosophical speculation and academic rhetoric. What is most important about the question, however, is the recognition that the personality and intuitive skills of the psychotherapist are as important as the technical knowledge and skills obtained from education and scientific training. Whatever the theoretical persuasion of the therapist, the most influential factor and common denominator of all psychotherapies lies in the personality of the therapist. Research and empirical observations indicate that the therapist's acceptance, warmth, and compassion are more crucial than his theoretical knowledge. This finding should in no way minimize the importance of adequate training and supervision, and a firm grasp of a theoretical framework from which to conduct therapy. In fact, we believe that the newly trained therapist is too often prone to minimize his skills because of a mistaken notion of modesty and a misinterpretation of the psychotherapeutic dictum to be humble and not too directive. For example, there is a tendency to over-emphasize the approach: "I'm not here to give advice. I don't have the answers." This approach can do much harm in diminishing the patient's confidence in the therapist's expertise. How would one feel if our physician told us that he does not have the knowledge to treat our physical ills? Caution must be taken to avoid minimizing the inherent therapeutic advantage and power that the therapist's status affords. The psychotherapist represents society's designated expert in helping and "curing" the emotionally troubled. To denigrate that expertise only reinforces the patient's sense of helplessness and takes away an important therapeutic asset of instilling hope and confidence.

THEORIES OF TREATMENT

There are numerous theoretical approaches to psychotherapy which are beyond the scope of this presentation. The bibliography contains a selective listing for those who are interested in further reading. Several obvious questions, however, do raise themselves. For instance, how necessary are theories? How are they useful? Are some theories better than others? How can one tell a bad theory from a good one? These questions are pertinent and legitimate, but not easily answered.

Regarding the necessity of theory, we firmly hold that a therapist must embrace and be guided by some theoretical framework to function effectively. Theory is synonymous with structure: a structure for comprehending what is going on. Without some such structure, anything a patient (or a therapist for that matter) might say or do becomes unintelligent and difficult to comprehend. All social interactions are guided by some theory or structure. Customs, mores, social roles, values, and philosophical systems are "theories" in that they provide a framework that allows us to explain, understand, and to some degree, predict the actions of ourselves and others. The usefulness of theory in everyday life, as well as for the professional psychotherapist, lies in this function: prediction and explanation. Without a theory, few of mankind's great achievements, from curing polio to sending a man to the moon, would have been possible.

Whether one theory is better, i.e., more effective, than another is an especially difficult and thorny question since it allies itself with some of the tribal, competitive, and destructive tendencies in both individuals and groups. Human beings are most prone to become habituated to what is familiar, comfortable, preserves the status quo, and does not rock the boat. To change to, or even consider, a new theory or theoretical modification is often a slow and arduous process, if not downright threatening. As psychotherapists, we should be aware of these pitfalls and dynamics, and avoid the fear of change and the destructive tendency to hold on rigidly to a fixed theory. Rather, we must seek out that which is usefully shared and common among many theories and avoid their divisive aspects. If man has learned anything from history, it is that no single philosophy or system of belief has ever been able to explain fully all of man's behavior and the phenomena of life around us. Even though we accept the sound scientific principle that the most effective and accurate theory is the one that offers the greatest economy (i.e., offers the most simple and least amount of explanations), we must be ever aware that no theory is *the* perfect theory and that theories live, evolve, and change.

If it is possible, therefore, to tell a good theory from a bad one, it would answer these questions: Does the theory, and the activity that proceeds from it, tend to ameliorate or encourage division and conflict? Is it flexible and open to change and modification, or is it closed and rigid? Perhaps, we also speak here not so much of schools of thought or theories, as we speak to individual clinicians and the manner in which they relate to whatever theoretical structures they have chosen. These are important questions which must be asked repeatedly of oneself. The tendency to solidify one's beliefs is stong and pervasive. Beware of it as it can only serve to reduce your effectiveness as a person and as a therapist.

The most important consideration in embracing a specific theoretical system is: how well does the theory fit the needs of the individual therapist? The answer to this reveals how well the therapist can relate and adapt theory to practice. In our experience, a therapist functions best with a theory that fits and complements his or her personal value system. When such is the case, clinical actions and reactions proceed more comfortably and naturally. In this sense, telling a bad theory from a good one evolves more realistically from what fits the individual therapist than from what is expedient, safe, or proper in some arbitrary, external manner. As an example, an extroverted and garrulous clinician might be ill-advised to consider classical psychoanalysis as a treatment modality as it would place restrictions on self-expression that could be difficult to reconcile over the protracted periods of time required by this technique. Conversely, an introverted and passive therapist would be ill-advised to attempt some of the group-oriented methods of treatment that demand spontaneous, physically active and outgoing behavior. (There are not many Fritz Perlses among us.) The issues and choices that flow from this consideration of the personality of the therapist in relation to methods cannot be overemphasized. For a therapist to work effectively, he must be comfortable and in full sympathy with his theoretical beliefs.

THE GOALS OF TREATMENT

The goals of therapy, together with the theoretical persuasion of the therapist, represent the sources of greatest influence on the treatment process. This may seem self-evident to the reader, but the authors' opinion is that its influence is often overlooked in the pressure of daily practice. One of the singular points that will be made continually throughout this presentation is the necessity of focusing and refocusing consistently on the several pivotal dynamics of psychotherapeutic work. Probably the most important focus that the therapist must maintain is an awareness of how his or her cognitive/affective traits affect therapy. Psychotherapy is an interactive process. It involves the interaction of the personalities of both patient *and* therapist. To a degree, the patient, by virtue of being the client and sufferer, is to be expected and even permitted to display an unfocused and irresponsible role. This "privilege" is denied to the professional. We are, to be sure, human and therefore fallible. Nevertheless, we have an uncommonly difficult responsibility: to be, as far as humanly possible, alert, honest, trustworthy, and ethical. It is a task we share with many other professions, only more so since psychotherapy can often have a crucial effect on the course of the patient's life.

What then are the goals of therapy? The answer to this basic question always comes from the patient. Listen to the patient and never forget what all patients seek in therapy: an alleviation of their suffering. Patients come to therapy to overcome their fears, doubts, and self-destructive behavior that have created sufficient anguish to prevent life from being satisfying and fulfilling. Patients want to know that you will help them. Troubled individuals want to feel that you can be sympathetic and accepting. Patients look for ways to fight their unhappiness. They seek understanding, advice, and direction that will lead to a happier and more fulfilled life. The psychotherapist should be ever mindful of these strivings so that he does not lose sight of the patient's suffering, and make therapy an intellectual, academic, or emotionally detached exercise. On the other hand, the patient's expectations, which are often desperate, should not lead the psychotherapist into being manipulated to become an advice-giver and to believe that he is an omnipotent and omniscient person. The therapist must always strive to achieve that balance between awareness of and confidence in his skills, and a realization of his limitations and lack of knowledge.

Arriving at a definition of therapeutic goals is not always the clear-cut and simple matter that the guidelines outlined above indicate. We refer to the common situation where the patient's presenting symptoms and expectations usually mask a more pertinent or underlying problem. This masking or evasion may be obvious to the therapist, but not to the patient. The therapist is frequently faced with these clinically, as well as ethically, ambiguous presenting situations. What can be done to clarify them to the patient without violating the patient's autonomy—and without violating his right to set goals? Furthermore, how does the therapist determine the difference between 1) maneuvering the patient to become what he does not want to be, however "good" it may be for him, and 2) aiding the patient to realize his potential for self-fulfillment and health without infringing on his freedom and individual rights?

The authors believe and practice psychotherapy based on the concept that the patient defines his own value systems and priorities within the framework of a specific social and cultural milieu. And that the ultimate potential and goal of psychotherapy is "to expand the domain of responsibility, authenticity, and integrity in the life of the patients." (Bloom, 1977, p. 335) There has been much controversy concerning the function of psychotherapists as social agents of the status quo. This discussion usually focuses around the accusation that the therapist serves to "adjust" patients to accept submissively the dominant social order without questioning the viability or appropriateness of the social system. To hold that this does not occur would be naive. To argue that it should never be allowed to occur is similarly naive. Psychotherapists, as well as their patients, represent a diverse cross-section of attitudes and values and there is bound to be at least some conflict with regard to this matter. Few therapists would argue (publicly, at any rate) that the ethical question of influencing and manipulating patients is not a real and serious concern. What the authors call for, then, is not a polemic on this issue as much as a caveat. It *is* happening. Psychotherapists *are* influencing patients' life-styles, and social and ethical values. Be aware of this and see how it can and does affect your practice. If you watch, you will see it operating both positively and negatively. Perhaps in no other profession does an awareness of the personal interaction between the professional and the client (provider and consumer) play such an important part in affecting the outcome of the process.

WHO SHOULD PRACTICE PSYCHOTHERAPY?

During the past decade, with its emphasis on "doing your thing," the age of Aquarius, the proliferation of innumerable encounter groups and meditative-type techniques telling us how to become happier and self-fulfilled, the concept of proper and sound psychotherapeutic training has been watered down. There appears to be a belief in our society today that anyone with an innovative idea or gimmick is a psychotherapist, especially in this age that wants to "do-it-yourself." Witness the huge success of how-to books and methods that promise the solutions of your hang-ups and insure instant happiness.

Because of the interpersonal, verbal, and emotional nature of therapy, laymen mistakenly believe that "anyone" can do psychotherapy. But, we believe that only the "anyone" who has received proper academic training, clinical training, and supervision is competent to engage in the practice of psychotherapy. The professions of psychology, psychiatry, and social work are chiefly responsible for turning out psychotherapists. A person who has completed formal training in any one of these disciplines and who meets the profession's accreditation standards for the practice of psychotherapy is on the threshold of being a therapist. What must follow, if one is to conduct psychotherapy, is a period of ongoing clinical supervision and/or training that is essentially didactic. Training institutes, postdoctoral programs, and some form of continuous personal clinical supervision best meet this criterion. Personal psychotherapy is an ideal that all potential therapists should undergo to understand the process of therapy, and more importantly, to become cognizant of one's own neurotic conflicts and defense mechanisms that influence our reactions to all people.

It is our strong conviction that the beginning psychotherapist should regularly see a "control" therapist who will supervise his practice. Supervision refers to the practice of the therapist bringing to the supervising therapist the innumerable problems of technique and philosophy that beset his practice. The control therapist's major function is two-fold: 1) to help the therapist develop more effective therapeutic skills and 2) to help the therapist become aware of his own idiosyncratic conflicts, inhibitions, and biases that can influence the outcome of therapy. For example, in a recent supervisory session, we were able to point out to the therapist trainee that his inability to develop satisfactory rapport and any therapeutic movement resulted from the countertransference. The therapist was reacting to the domineering manner and provoking remarks of a middle-aged woman in the same way he handled this typical behavior of his mother: toward his mother, as with the patient, he reacted with a passive, withdrawn, and uninvolved attitude. This supervisory relationship is of immense value not only to the newly-trained psychotherapist, but for the experienced professional who serves as a control. Being a control therapist enables you to keep on top of your technique and underlying limitations that affect psychotherapy, and also provides a more objective evaluation of your diagnostic and treatment skills than can be gained from a self-evaluation.

To treat people in psychotherapy is to be confronted daily with profound discontent, misery, rage, and helplessness. To cope effectively with this barrage of negative human emotions requires all the understanding and personal stability that we, the therapists, can muster. Personal psychotherapy and ongoing supervision represent the best training methods to help us achieve this understanding. Being a good therapist is a skill that can be learned. The idea that good therapists are born and not made is fallacious. Perhaps *great* therapists are born, but competency and success remains, as Edison noted, more perspiration than inspiration. Beyond these technical skills, we assume that every psychotherapist brings a much-needed and deep commitment to his work, a dedication, a certain altruism, if you will, to help others. This commitment or altruism, however, must be tempered with a strong dose of realism and humility.

THE LIMITATIONS OF THERAPY

That the practice of psychotherapy is beset with certain limiting factors is implied from the foregoing discussion. Very real and sometimes unavoidable limitations operate when practicing therapy. Probably the greatest and most significant limitation is the ability or skill of the therapist. The plain fact is that some people make better therapists than others. Numerous research studies on treatment efficacy seem to agree consistently on this issue (Stollak, 1966). Whereas there tends to be only small and nonsignificant differences between the results of the various technical therapeutic methods, there are real and significant differences between individual therapists. Attempts to isolate and define these differences disclose that no matter what the therapeutic approach, successful therapists tend to be similar to each other even across lines of doctrine and technique (Goldstein, 1962). These results are far from conclusive, however, as differing personality types can be as yet only crudely delineated. Moreover, even when identified (e.g., Type A, distant/authoritarian, Type B, warm/permissive, Loor, 1964; Tyler 1964) there is a further breakdown into successful and unsuccessful within these categories (Moos 1967).

The second limiting condition of therapy resides within the patient. Not every patient will improve. Some, in fact, may deteriorate, despite our best efforts, and, more pertinent, not every patient will work optimally with every therapist. The pressures of clinical practice do not allow unlimited access to a broad selection of potential therapists or patients. Consequently, the average professional and patient often find themselves working under less than ideal circumstances and without clear guidelines to identify this situation. Given these factors, it is important that the therapist know both his own and the patient's limitations. The ability to discern the difference between a temporary and a permanent impasse increases with skill and experience. Here, as with most questions of technique, appropriate supervision will be the key factor in clarifying your doubts. Often it is difficult, if not impossible, for the novice therapist to distinguish between the two, and the more skilled and less biased insight of the supervisor will help provide clarification.

Patients also bring other restrictions and obstacles to therapy such as poor motivation, less ego strength, and less proclivity to relate to psychotherapy than others. In addition, some will react to whatever approach the clinician uses with varying degrees of adaptability. Being aware of these restricting factors allows one to modify the goals and methods of therapy to fit the individual circumstance. Every therapist must also come to terms with the realization that some patients will never improve, or will improve only up to a certain point. A few will require long-term maintenance. Still other patients must be immediately or eventually referred to another therapist or other kinds of treatment due to the limitations that exist in your relationship. Deciding whether a patient is capable of engaging in the minimum effort required for viable treatment is often difficult and requires a thorough understanding of all the factors that exist to restrict your therapeutic effectiveness.

A third limitation is a corollary of the above since it involves the interaction of patient and therapist even under optimal conditions of rapport. This is the limitation imposed by the treatment methods and theoretical structure of the therapist. All treatment approaches are, to a greater or lesser degree, self-limiting. Short-term and crisis-intervention therapies have inherent temporal limits and their goals must be modified to fit these parameters. Behavioral therapies are likewise often confined both in time and the complexity of issues which they address. Behavioral approaches direct their attention to symptom removal and focus on conditioning methods as opposed to exploring personality dynamics. Psychoanalytically-oriented methods, which seek to uncover the influence of unconscious motivation and historical antecedents, require a longer time in therapy, and the ability and readiness of the patient to work at a more intensive level of personal scrutiny than most other

treatment approaches. Being vigilantly aware of the require-
ments of your theoretical system and therapeutic techniques
will enable you to better understand the limiting factors that
exist in the therapeutic interaction.

ETHICAL CONSIDERATIONS

Although the ethics of practicing psychotherapy is a topic
that can be discussed under the limitations of therapy, its importance demands special mention. In recent years, there has
been a growing awareness of the enormous importance of the
psychotherapist's conduct in the therapeutic relationship. The
ethics and moral values of the psychotherapist is a topic that
is finally receiving a long overdue scrutiny. The traditional
stereotype of the psychotherapist as a detached, uninvolved,
and objective expert is being recognized as a one-sided and
incomplete characterization of the therapist's level of involvement with the patient. It is becoming increasingly clear that the
therapist's behavior and value system represent important influences and models for the patient. Therefore, psychotherapists
must be ever mindful of maintaining the highest degree of
ethical practices. The temptation to indulge our neurotic conflicts and impulses is always with us. The patient can easily be
taken advantage of under the guise of good therapeutic intentions.

One of the most flagrant abuses that a therapist can display
is to encourage or accede to a sexual relationship with a patient.
This is usually rationalized as providing much-needed love and
support to an emotionally deprived client. Such behavior can
only be viewed as professional misconduct and quite unethical.
Whatever a therapist does to impose his behavior and needs
onto a patient can only harm that person and the therapeutic
process. In the case of a sexual affair with a patient, the psychotherapist is essentially gratifying narcissistic needs at the expense of a patient's chance for healthy growth. What is a patient
to think and feel about a therapist who is susceptible to the

patient's fantasies and impulses? Therapists need be ever cognizant of the client's manipulative behavior that can take on many subtle forms. Recently, for example, a patient asked whether the therapist would be willing to take five dollars less per session if he paid in cash. Agreeing to this, like any other manipulation, would be falling into his neurotic (and, in this case, also unethical) pattern, and reinforcing the patient's inappropriate way of dealing with life.

Maintaining and respecting confidentiality is nowhere more crucial and mandatory than in a therapeutic relationship. In our age where individual privacy is constantly threatened, invaded, and infringed upon by society's mania for record keeping, psychotherapy stands as one of the few professions that must maintain the individual's confidences. For without trust between the therapist and patient little will be accomplished. The authors subscribe to the idea that no information, which the patient has provided the therapist, can be divulged to anyone unless the patient gives permission. Specifically, we refer to direct requests from parents, mates, friends, relatives, employers, and other professionals including schools, agencies, and hospitals. Before such permission is given, the patient should know and understand the reason(s) for a request for information. Moreover, we believe the therapist should fully share with the patient the content of the report or information that is given or prepared for someone. Therapists must, at all costs, respect a person's confidence. To betray a confidence is a violation of trust. And such violations will only impair the ability of the therapist to help a suffering human being. As Max Siegel (1977, p. 6) recently noted, in over 35 years of practive "my clinical failures were most often associated with an absence of mutual respect and trust, and my successes with complete, unequivocal acceptance and trust." Even in situations which present the possibility of potential danger, Dr. Siegel would never betray a confidence, although he would do everything possible to protect a life. Extreme as this view of confidentiality appears, it is the position that every therapist should strive to emulate.

As a social agent and a highly significant and symbolic

figure, the therapist is capable of exerting a powerful influence over those with whom he works. This power is considerable and like all power may be used constructively or destructively depending upon the individual wielding it. From time to time, reports appear in the press attesting to the various abuses of this power, alleged or substantiated. Although the variety and extent of these abuses are open to debate, there is no doubt that they exist. We, as psychotherapists, must be continually reminded of the necessity for thorough training, preparation, and supervision, and the highest standards of ethical conduct. This cannot be emphasized too strongly since psychotherapy deals with the very foundation of human values and attitudes. The ethical conduct of the therapist will never be questioned if his behavior and techniques remain compatible with the goals of health, personal growth, and respect for the patient's autonomy.

This beginning chapter has attempted to give a general overview of some of the issues within psychotherapy and to acquaint the reader with our basic outlook. We view therapy as a holistic, interactive, and integrative process. The therapist is not, or should not be a cloistered specialist, remote, and hiding behind his expert status, desk, or lab coat. She or he is merely another individual, however highly trained, bringing to the therapeutic encounter both that training and distinctive attributes as a person. The patient, who is not "ill" in the same sense that a medical patient is physically ill, also brings his background and needs to therapy. This is the raw material of psychotherapy. If we appear simplistic, perhaps it is because the idea of therapy, like the idea of life, is simple. The complexities are the invention of the individuals involved and these can be formidable. A psychotherapist would do well to remind himself every day that it is the simplicity that is to be sought, not the complexity. The complex tends to obscure and the simple clarifies. So read the following with an eye for simplicity. It will make a difference.

Chapter 2

THE PATIENT AS A PERSON

Within the working life of every psychotherapist, an unusual event will occur: the encounter with a new patient. This event can be described as singular, despite the fact that it will happen hundreds and perhaps thousands of times. This patient, by whatever circumstances he or she comes to you, is troubled enough to have made a most difficult and even courageous decision to seek assistance with his life. This decision is a momentous one for the patient. No other decision is quite the same, whether it be legal, financial, or medical, since the person usually feels not so much the need for an expert opinion as he feels a helplessness and failure. In our culture, the average individual does not expect to be expert in the law or medicine. He does, however, usually expect to be able to deal with his everyday problems. Added to this is the still common stigma of being "crazy" or "sick" that attaches itself to being in therapy. As a result, there is almost always an aura of fear, shame, and reluctance associated with seeking psychotherapy.

The therapist must be aware of these factors as he confronts the new patient. He will, in fact, be examining the posture, attitude, and behavior for clues to the particular problems that will need to be dealt with. At the onset, then, there are several important differences between the two participants. Differences that will color the interaction and render the work more difficult if the therapist is not attuned to them and, in effect, forewarned.

To begin with, there are relatively few therapists and many patients. For a particular therapist, an individual may be interview number 10 or number 1,000. Yet for the patient, the therapist is usually the first, or at most, the second or third therapeutic contact. This is not really a trivial point. Hopefully, the primary difference between the hundredth patient and the thousandth patient is experience and expertise. Under pressures of time and workload, there is a great temptation to perceive patients as "cases" and "sessions." It is not uncommon for patients to express the fear that to the therapist they are only "John Smith, 3:00 P.M., Thursday," not a human being, but a time slot and a number. This fear is real and virtually omnipresent. That the therapist has worked with them for months or years and does not have nor ever gives concrete evidence of such an attitude does not matter. We live in a capitalistic society and patients (or third-parties) pay us, and were we not paid, the chances are great that we would not continue to see them.

This is one of the dilemmas of psychotherapy. It is a consumer relationship with a person who needs a personal relationship. (For it is a truism that the individual without serious flaws in his basic ability to relate positively and with significance to others is seldom seen in treatment.) The therapist must therefore begin work in a somewhat contradictory situation. He or she must develop a helping relationship with the patient within parameters that can seriously limit the potential ability of both parties to relate under the rules and roles dictated by the surrounding culture. Yet, above all, the patient is a person, a unique individual who must be seen in a personal and individual context. To see a patient as a case, rather than as a suffering person, would vitiate the development of a constructive relationship by reenforcing the distance and difficulties in communication that underlie the very reason for seeking assistance.

On the other hand, the therapist's basic tools involve his separation from and objectivity to the patient's distress. One cannot become embroiled in the patient's personal life and still hope to be effective. Such is the therapist's (and patient's) dilemma. We should convey a full measure of interest and human concern, yet we cannot love, take care of, or identify with his problems to the point of becoming emotionally involved. To do so would cloud our judgment. It is a difficult balancing act; one that grows easier with experience and good supervision, but a relationship that always remains a challenge.

It is important to know that there is no patient who will not affect you in some way, positively, negatively, or both; or that will not provoke some countertransference. At this point, all we can do is to be continually conscious of this reality and its signals. If the therapist is open to listen to these messages, they will teach him a great deal about himself and his patients.

WHY PEOPLE SEEK TREATMENT

There is one basic reason that brings someone to a psychotherapist. The consciousness that he can no longer deal effectively with a major part of life; or the awareness that he can no longer maintain the fiction that he *is* dealing effectively with some important aspect of his life. A common variation is that some significant person (spouse, parent, friend, employer) has convinced or coerced the individual into acknowledging his ineffectiveness. Therefore, the question: "What brings you to therapy?" should be the first order of business. The answer to this first question is of the utmost significance. Whether it is clear or vague, straightforward or oblique, it will communicate a great deal about the patient and his or her approach to treatment. As such, the clinician listens carefully and with a clear and open mind to the response with its implicit and explicit connotations.

As therapists, we must take special care to realize that there is a powerful tendency in all human beings to seek answers. When confronting the new patient the novice therapist is most highly stressed. This is it! This is what our long and exacting training has prepared us for. This is the therapist's moment of truth: the therapeutic encounter with a patient. You will be nervous, pressured, and most probably feel afraid and inadequate. This is natural, usual, and to be expected. Somehow, in spite of everything, you will be able to function and get through. One might as well become used to it. It may be years before the anxiety goes away completely, if it ever does. This is the "stage-fright" of psychotherapy and we all have had it. The inherent danger in this normal anxiety lies in a tendency to seek answers—not for the patient—but to quiet our own fears. This is the danger of snap judgment and facile categorization, without getting to know the patient as a suffering individual. However classical and obvious the symptomology may appear, the therapist must beware of this temptation, especially the beginning therapist with the new patient. Each person with whom we work is unique, so unique that he will never fit exactly any diagnostic category or any theoretical rubric. The pressure placed upon the clinician both by himself, his training, and indirectly by the patient to pigeon-hole and classify is strong and constant. To avoid becoming a mere technician and a faulty one at that, the pressure to categorize must be consciously resisted. This is imperative, if for no other reason than our techniques are still imperfect. Furthermore, because easy generalizations tend to diminish the humanity of the participants and the process as a whole. Instead of quick judgments, there should be observation and interaction, seeing and listening, both with the patient and with one's self. Enough emphasis cannot be placed on this basic precept of psychotherapy. The patient must not be fitted to our awareness, rather, our awareness must be fitted to the patient. Yet this does not minimize the great importance of precise diagnostic understanding and formulation of the patient's problems, a topic to be explored later.

THE EXPECTATIONS OF THE PATIENT

People seen in psychotherapy represent the entire range of backgrounds and life experiences. While the therapist must be prepared to deal with the broad spectrum, certain age, socioeconomic, and ethnic groups will tend to be overrepresented. This mix of patients will vary with the geographic location of the therapist. Therapists should be knowledgeable about the demographic characteristics of one's area of practice. For the most part, patients in private practice tend to be white and lower-middle to upper-middle class. Clinic and/or institutional practice can be quite different, however, depending on various demographic factors. These differing groups tend to have somewhat varying expectations.

Aside from these differences, a certain commonality of expectation exists. Basically, the patient expects to be helped with whatever problem or perception of problem he or she has. Patients must feel "helped" for effective therapy to take place. If treatment does not help and is not felt useful, there would be little justification for continuing, and small likelihood of success, even if therapy continued. Clinicians must repeatedly ask the question, "is this treatment useful to the patient?" This utility must, above all, be experienced by the patient. As simple as this may seem, this issue is often lost sight of in the routine of everyday practice. Keep in mind to ask yourself *and the patient,* from time to time, whether this requirement is being satisfied. It is an indispensable aspect of the focusing of issues continually necessary for effective therapy.

Another primary expectation of the patient is that the therapist be competent, knowledgeable, and qualified. Were this not the case, the patient would be wasting time and money. Those readers who are beginning therapists may experience some degree of doubt as to their competency and qualification. At least the authors *hope* that this possibility will cross the reader's mind. There are few professions where a healthy sense of humility and self-examination is so pertinent and productive. At no time should the individual being treated feel that the practitioner is unqualified, incompetent, or out of control. This, of course, places a burden on the novice therapist who must function as if he were feeling competent when, in fact, he may not be feeling particularly competent at that moment. Our suggestion is to be aware of what is happening and relax. We have all been through it and most have survived. Often, it helps to remember that although the patient may have unrealistic expectations as to our power and expertise, he also tends to resolve "the benefit of doubt" most often in our favor. We say this not to encourage complacency, but to place a predictable anxiety in better perspective.

An extension of this patient expectation is a common one: that therapists have almost magical powers. Specifically, that therapists can perceive what the patient is experiencing, but not communicating; that we have access to special techniques that will "cure"; that we inexplicably withhold this special knowledge and power for vague reasons (which in the patient's eyes tend to revolve around our personal feelings towards him) and that we can and should take the major responsibility and effort to cure the patient. Obviously, these issues all relate to transference phenomena, as opposed to the first two expectations cited, which are realistic and fully warranted, within limits. Nevertheless, they are important factors of the treatment process. It is a somewhat sad truth that few, if any, of our patients will ever see us *except* through a highly distorted and symbolic perception. Whereas, it is of the utmost importance for the clinician to see the patient as a person, the therapist must accept the likelihood that patients will seldom, if ever, return the compliment. This is the nature of the relationship and a kind of loneliness that comes with the territory.

Another major expectation that most patients bring to therapy is that of making direct, personal contact with the therapist together with a desire to know about the therapist as a person beyond his or her professional attributes and capabilities (Rogers & Dymond, 1964). This is a common phenomenon of the general set of expectations each person brings to his encounters with others. Here again, there is a delicate balance to be observed by the practitioner in handling the situation. Transference and symbolic issues will color the interaction greatly. The need to make meaningful contact with the clinician is both genuine and therapeutically useful. If it does not exist, the therapeutic alliance may never be joined and the motivation to work and grow remain untapped.

A stereotype exists in the public mind that characterizes psychotherapists as aloof, distant, and personally inaccessible. This is unfortunate and probably resulted from the tendency of classically trained psychoanalysts to take a passive and enigmatic role, saying little and refusing to discuss themselves in treatment. A more or less convincing theoretical case can be made for this stance in psychoanalysis. Today, however, the social and clinical environment has changed considerably from that of Freud's time. The majority of therapists and patients are not practicing orthodox or classical psychoanalysis. It is our view that the therapist should be prepared to encounter the patient directly as one person to another. Therefore, personal questions may be answered within reason and as seem appropriate. A patient will understandably feel a certain unfairness about someone asking and knowing so much about his personal life while he cannot know anything about the inquirer. For the therapist to refuse rigidly to respond to questions will only tend to reenforce the magical thinking of the patient. In our experience, patients will usually be satisfied with brief and straightforward responses to queries about age, background, schooling, marital status, where and how one lives, etc. Like all therapeutic interaction, the manner and content of the questions and the patient's response to the answers will provide much useful information. It is not usually difficult for the clinician to gauge his response and what to disclose. A natural answer will almost always suffice, but the patient must be informed that the focus of a session concerns information about the patient, not the therapist. Answering questions, however, will frequently make the patient feel more at ease and less apt to engage in useless speculation about the therapist. Most important, the therapist must evaluate and understand the reasons for the patient's inquiries about the therapist. Do the questions reflect natural curiosity or a need to manipulate, control, evade, or seek attention? The answer to this will provide the therapist with important clues about the patient's personality functioning and dynamics. The topic will be further explored in our later discussion of the initial consultation.

The patient's expectation for guidance and direction is the final example of what one expects from psychotherapy. *All* patients expect advice and counsel, even if they know that it is not the major purpose of therapy. Again, it is difficult to formulate hard and fast guidelines for when and when not to be directive and offer advice. We do feel, however, that it is poor practice to either *always* or *never* engage in such behavior. A good deal will depend upon the individual circumstance, but some broad outline may be helpful. It is seldom, if ever, warranted to refrain from making a direct intervention when the patient presents a clear physical danger to himself or to someone else. Patently destructive behavior should be noted and confronted. Here again, a balance must be struck between whatever complications might arise from intervention and the risks inherent in the destructive behavior. Keep in mind that there is a tacit complicity in the behavior through nonintervention. For now, it is only necessary to consider the concept of balance. Skills will develop with experience and good supervision.

THE RIGHTS OF PATIENTS

Patients have certain clear rights and privileges. They have, most pertinently, the right to our total, undivided attention and professional concern. The first duty of the clinician is to listen and observe. Patients have the right to their own idiosyncratic attitudes and values and the perceptions and actions that flow from these. One of the most difficult tasks a therapist will face is to distinguish between "disturbed" behavior and legitimate individual difference in life-style. The authors strongly believe that the therapist has no right or obligation to function as an agent of the status quo of society by pressuring, however subtly, the patient to adjust to conventional mores and modes of conduct. The patient has the right to be seen as an individual, a discrete and separate personality, not another "case." This emphasis on the patient's individuality, as well as with many of the ideas already stressed, appears self-evident. In practice, however, such basic concepts can be all too easily overlooked. These are the basics of therapy on which the therapist must constantly focus and refocus.

Another right of the patient is the right to be respected and treated equally with all other patients. This may, on occasion, be a difficult task for the therapist since patients present disordered and bizarre behavior that will conflict with the socially conditioned value judgments to which all people, including therapists, are subject. The social conditioning of the therapist strongly influences his notions of superiority/inferiority, adequacy/inadequacy, and competence/incompetence in human relations. Consequently, the clinician may be prone to view his role as being "superior," especially when he has not examined his own power and status needs. Unfortunately, the patient will often reenforce this perception by his helpless stance. Viewing your therapeutic role as a power base is not only unethical, but harmful. It operates to reenforce the patient's negative self-perceptions which constitute the core of problems for which therapy is being sought. Although it is inevitable that we will react more favorably to some personality types than others, the therapist must be aware that this is a luxury of personal freedom that cannot be followed as freely in one's profession as in one's private life. For example, we can quickly choose to have nothing further to do with a new acquaintance who is a bore. This is not so easily done in therapy.

As a general rule, which bears directly on this occasional dilemma, we submit that it is wise to decline to take on a patient who arouses a strong dislike in us. We further suggest that, in order to devlop a sense of comfort with a patient, the clinician cultivate the ability to find or select one aspect of the patient's behavior that can be genuinely appreciated and respected. If this cannot be done, (and it is the authors' experience that it is the rare patient with whom it cannot be done) it strongly indicates that little, if anything, will be accomplished with that person.

A final patient right is to be treated with the highest ethical conduct from the therapist. Patients must be told the truth. How the truth is told is a matter of judgment and technique. That it *must* be told is never an issue. Beyond the ethical considerations, we hold this position for quite practical reasons. If the patient should ever discover a therapist's deception (and chances are that they will), the likelihood of continued effective treatment would be greatly reduced or, more probably, totally destroyed. For this reason, it is best for the novice therapist to confront this issue from the onset of his clinical work. There will be temptations. At times, it will seem that a "little white lie" would be supportive or ego-enhancing, or "grease the wheels" of therapy. This never is so. Progress based upon false premises, however well-intentioned, will disintegrate when the falsehood is discovered. In addition, many patients have been regularly lied to for various purposes by parents and other significant figures. Usually, many have fallen into this trap of self-deception out of fear or contempt. Consequently, they will continue this same game with the therapist, often weaving a hopelessly tangled web before the pattern can be uncovered. On every level, the potential disaster of this practice far outweighs the potential gain. Avoid any semblance of distorting the truth and practicing deception of any kind.

The need for ethical conduct in other areas of therapeutic interaction is clear and obvious. The therapist bears a responsibility to refrain from financially exploiting the patient. This includes not only fees, but also gaining benefits from the patient because of his position of influence. Finally, as noted in the public press recently, the problem of sexual contact with patients is constantly with us. The authors believe that sexual relations with patients is patently unethical and has no therapeutic value. Every clinician will on occasion be directly or indirectly approached sexually by those he treats. Therefore, each therapist must be aware of his sexual adjustment and how his needs are being fulfilled.* This awareness will provide a kind of "insurance" against this inevitable temptation. Our patients are not there to gratify our needs any more than we are there to gratify their needs. We practice for fees to earn a livelihood. More important, we practice for the personal satisfaction of competently performing useful and honorable work. No dollar value can be placed on this. It is a priceless possession.

THE PATIENT'S TASKS AND OBLIGATIONS

Rights and privileges imply tasks and obligations. The tasks and obligations of the patient are simple, but important. The first and most obvious is that the patient must come to his appointments. If he does not come, we cannot help him. This must be clearly and unequivocally stated from the beginning. It is a condition of accepting a person into treatment. Second, the patient must be prepared, on some level, to engage in a

---

*The limited studies on this topic conclude that those therapists involved in sexual relations with patients appear to be undergoing a period of deprivation in their personal relations and sexual lives (Dahlberg, 1970; Van Emde, 1966).

minimum of therapeutic work. This is a difficult issue to define and one that will be expanded on in the chapter discussing beginning therapy. In a certain sense, it is the responsibility of the therapist to help the patient in developing his ability to engage in therapy. Although the patient must essentially accomplish the task on his own, our point is that the therapist can help make him ready for therapy.

We, as therapists, are assisted in this task by a fundamental assumption. Stated in different ways by different theorists, this underlying assumption posits the existence of a drive or force within the patient that seeks health, growth, and productive functioning. Each practitioner must find, through all the barriers thrown up by the patient and the pathology of the surrounding culture, some way of allying ourselves with this force—whatever we name it or conceive it to be. A constant questioning must go on in the clinician's mind: "What are the positive forces in this person's make-up? How can I discover, contact, evoke, and clarify them? What can be done to increase their presence in the patient's life?" These basic and simple questions, asked over and over, about the specific patient, will aid the clinician in focusing on a direction to take in most situations.

Beyond these issues are some of a more mundane nature. The patient has the obligation to pay the fee agreed upon (if fees are involved in the setting). It is the rare patient who would not rather pay less and the rare professional who would not rather earn more. It is important that the patient pay no more than he can manage realistically, and that the therapist does not feel he is receiving less than he deserves. Striking that balance is not always easy and the practitioner will often wish that he did not have to deal with it. For guidelines, consult your own ego and super-ego besides the fee rates in your area. Keep in mind, however, that if you feel you are charging either too much or too little, this is an important issue to be resolved. Unresolved, it will inevitably have a measurably negative effect on your work. The overriding consideration in establishing a fee is to be sensitive to the needs of the patient's ego so that his self-esteem is not threatened or attacked.

THE THERAPEUTIC CONTRACT

Many of the issues discussed thus far have related directly to the concept of the therapeutic contract. Most theoreticians and clinical practitioners have spoken implicitly or explicitly about the notion of the contract in psychotherapy (Feifel & Ells, 1963; Strupp, 1969; Truax, 1963). The authors view this as an important issue and subsume it under our ideas about the importance of focusing and refocusing throughout the therapeutic process. As soon as the initial intake and diagnostic consultations are completed, the participants must come to an agreement: whether or not to work together. As soon as this agreement is reached, they must define what this work will involve. This definition should include some statement and agreement about the patient's problem, why treatment was sought, and the rights and tasks of each party. It should also include some clarification of the expectations of the parties: what methods the therapist intends to use and what specific and general goals are set. This, in effect, is the contract. Although establishing a contractual agreement is a proper and sensible thing to do, you may find it surprisingly difficult to do consistently with each new patient. You will find yourself forgetting or making excuses for putting if off. But, it is a discipline that will pay off handsomely in increased effectiveness and efficiency.

This contract is continually open to change and renegotiation during the course of treatment and should be clear to the patient and therapist. Change is not unusual and should be expected. Though the therapeutic interaction may drift from week to week and topic to topic, this is not the planned change to which we refer. Patients, for instance, will often wish to concentrate on some specific current incident or crisis. It is all too easy to respond to the immediate situation, especially if it is highly charged. This is not to say that these immediate issues are to be ignored in favor of a rigidly defined treatment plan. The test of the therapist's skill will lie in being able to relate the prevailing situation to the overall goal and plan of therapy. Working with many patients from week to week, the therapist will understandably have difficulty in maintaining a consistent and different focus with each, especially in the face of the direct crises that arise in each patient's daily life. Furthermore, we must keep in mind that the habitual negative patterns in the patient's make-up will attempt to maintain themselves and lead the therapeutic encounter away from confronting the focal problems and issues. The obligation falls on the clinician, then, to focus and refocus on the contract and maintain a specific and relevant direction.

Chapter 3

THE THERAPIST AS A PERSON

In the preceding chapter, we discussed some of the aspects and characteristics of the principal focus of psychotherapy: the patient. It seems appropriate, therefore, to say something about the therapist, the other participant in the process. Several broad issues need to be considered. How and why, for instance, do certain individuals become psychotherapists? How are psychotherapists seen by the public? What is it like to be a therapist? What characterizes a good therapist, and how does being a therapist influence and affect one as a person?

The preconceptions people bring to the therapeutic encounter, as professionals or laymen, will influence the resulting interaction and outcome. Whatever these preconceptions may be, psychotherapy is a human activity engaged in by human beings in a relatively ambiguous human context. As such, it has more in common with education, religion, and the law than with more precise technical disciplines like chemistry or engineering. The influence of personal variables, therefore, on the practice of therapy is of pivotal importance. There is little that can be firmly proved or accurately quantified, and much that must be accepted and assumed. Intuition plays as important a role as technical training. What the participants "feel" about what is occurring can be, and often is, more important than what the objective or relevant issues might be. Let us consider, then, something of the therapist as a person.

How People Become Psychotherapists

Anyone who has had acquaintance with a sample of graduate students in training to become clinicians is familiar with their persistent complaints about the irrelevance of their studies with regard to what they will be doing as mental health practitioners. Often it seems that that there are two "tasks" to be performed. The first concerns mastering the academic skills necessary to compete for and become eligible for graduate education. The second task is to learn enough about the practicalities and realities of everyday practice so that you can function as a clinician after completing your training. Complaints about relevancy usually refer to the gap or disparity between these two tasks. Ideally, they should be identical or at least as similar as possible. Realistically, they can be quite different and separate.

For the most part, formal education is an academic and intellectual process. It rewards perseverance, memory, verbal skills, and abstract reasoning. It rewards most frequently the introverted and obsessive personality who can submit his personal, physical, and social needs to the asceticism of disciplined work and study. There may be exceptions to this rule, but for the majority it holds true. Most of us, therefore, come to our profession through an exacting process of selection. Those who resisted or were unable to cope with the traditional pedagogical methods were discouraged or dropped. "Objective" information was promulgated as being superior to "subjective" experience. We were exhorted to "go along with the program."

There is a cynical saying among graduate students: "You are not allowed to have an opinion about anything until you complete your degree. By then, you no longer have any opinions." The academic philosophy behind this sarcasm is often defended as a necessary discipline. More frequently, however, it can merely be an expression of the authoritarian needs of the various members of the institutions involved. The problem with this approach is, as McLuhan (1964) has noted that the medium can become the message. The abstract, rigid, and scientific-intellectual biases of academic training spill over into a pervasive attitude in those being trained that can influence their later professional work by negating the importance of intuition or subjective experience. We do not mean to imply that academic preparation is without value, however, one needs to take a fresh look at its hidden messages. Psychotherapy is both an ancient discipline (preliterate societies' emphasis on faith healing), and an infant science. There is yet the need to emphasize that there should be a merging of academic and practical daily skills that recognize a subjective basis. Academic preparation can and should provide a coherent superstructure within which to work. It does not, however, provide much more than an abstract notion of the skills necessary to be a good clinician. Moreover, it tends to compete with the development of those invaluable social, interpersonal skills of perception and intuition that are invaluable to becoming an effective therapist.

Every beginning psychotherapist should ask himself questions of a soul-searching nature such as: "How do I relate to people?" "How do I relate to myself?" "How do I see myself?" "How satisfactory are my close personal relationships?" "What work remains to be done in overcoming my own conflicts and neurotic (ineffective) behavior?" The conventional medium for the novice clinician in dealing with personal problems should involve a period of psychotherapy. As with our patients, this idea may arouse fear, shame, and resistance. Consider, however, that not only is it an unavoidable responsibility, but, if necessary, we have the soothing rationalization that it is "only for our professional development." This will help you over the rough spots at the beginning until you can become more immediately engaged in the same valuable process that you, after all, will be trying to sell to others. The authors have never met a therapist who did not agree that he needed the therapy he has had, or who could not have used some if he had not. Our point is that there are certain clear, negative aspects to the usual academic selection and indoctrination processes. Let us be candid about this and search out their effects in ourselves and take whatever steps are necessary to correct them.

WHY PEOPLE BECOME PSYCHOTHERAPISTS

This is an interesting and relevant question which each therapist should ask himself and answer honestly. As already noted, each therapist expresses and satisfies many personal needs through his work. During undergraduate days the common reaction was that all psychology majors were "disturbed," and that this was their basic reason for choosing the major. Like most folk wisdom, this contains more than a germ of truth. Whenever a person deliberately and consciously chooses a field of specialization it would appear reasonable to conclude that this interest is usually grounded in some deep inner need, which may be more or less concealed. Whether becoming therapists arises from an attempt to resolve our personal turmoil, from an altruistic desire to help others, from needs for prestige or financial security, or from some combination of these needs is irrelevant unless the basis of this motivation is fraught with conflict. In addition to these acceptable needs, the need for power and dominance is potentially destructive. Since any person who aspires to be a psychotherapist is seeking a position that implies a degree of personal power over the lives of others, this is an aspect that requires examination.

Psychotherapists are granted a certain authority and the status of expert in our society. This authority is further enhanced by both the mythology surrounding doctors and the effect of transferential factors in the psychotherapeutic relationship. Patients, for the most part, expect (or hope) that their therapist will be a wise and powerful person. This expectation will often lead the patient to overlook any evidence of personal or professional weaknesses, or to be hypersensitive to any hint of human failing. These distortions are usual and to be expected. Our concern is with the potential abuse of these distortions by the therapist. It is not always easy to maintain a healthy sense of proportion about one's own abilities and failings while practicing psychotherapy. In the beginning stages especially, the novice therapist will often find himself vascillating between feelings of inadequacy and failure with difficult and negative patients, and euphoria and omnipotence with those who are responsive and admiring. We are reminded here of some of Berne's (1969) acute observations about the game of "psychiatry." Often those you work with will act out variations of "Why aren't you helping me?" or "Gee you're wonderful, Doctor!" Depending upon our state of self-perception at the moment, we may be inclined to believe one opinion or the other at a given moment. All things considered, however, most of us would rather believe (or have others believe) that we are wonderful.

There is a natural, if generally unconscious, tendency in most people to withdraw from and devalue negative response from others and gravitate towards and reenforce positive reactions. Any sense of inadequacy and guilt that will arise from negative interaction will tend to push a clinician towards patients who react positively to him. A clear understanding is needed that neither response is more intrinsically accurate or true than the other. Given the pressures acting upon every novice psychotherapist, it is imperative to be cognizant of this situation and learn how to deal with it before a set of bad habits becomes ingrained in your clinical technique. By bad habits, in this instance, we mean the propensity to reward positive and punish negative reactions to the therapist.

A successful clinician must necessarily have a good opinion of his or her therapeutic skills and abilities. This opinion, however, should not rest substantially upon the adoration of one's patients. Unfortunately, we can think of instances among colleagues where the virtue of self-assurance has apparently crossed the boundary into the vice of a self-serving arrogance and egomania. Imposing this type of attitude and behavior on one's peers is merely bad taste or poor judgment. To exhibit it to patients under your care is a violation of our trust as therapists and a vitiation of our potential as healing agents. Incidentally, we feel this arrogant and patronizing attitude is responsible, to some degree, for much of the negative public image of psychotherapy and psychotherapists. As we list a few of the more obvious examples, the reader may smile or wince in recognition of these as they may apply to himself or others:

1. Being an "originator" or zealous adherent to the "best," "only true," "most dynamic," or "soon to be dominant" school or technique of treatment.
2. The therapist who has "senior" patients who run groups or "take over" for him during vacations or other absences.
3. A practitioner who "trains" individuals from his caseload while continuing as the therapist.
4. A therapist who structures or encourages extra-therapeutic socializing with some or all of his current patient population. (Often rationalized as being "more human" or as "reducing therapeutic distance." Usually this is merely to obtain a circle of admirers to insulate the therapist from his own social inadequacies.)
5. The therapist who establishes a "therapeutic community" that provides an extensive ongoing "protective environment" for his patients as a substitute for a social life outside of the therapeutic milieu. (This is to be distinguished from programs deliberately set up as

therapeutic communities for a population selected and identified as having serious social handicaps as a condition of entering the setting.)

6. The therapist whose "busy schedule" of activities tends to frequently take time from regularly scheduled appointments.
7. Any treatment method that encourages its participants to perceive of themselves as "different," "better," "misunderstood" as the reason for being unable to relate to others.
8. Asking favors of patients or using them for errands, odd jobs, or personal projects.
9. The clinician who regularly disparages, ridicules, or in other ways shows contempt for the disordered behavior of patients.

The "cult of the personality" is no stranger to psychotherapeutic history. Some of the most widely-known public figures in the field may fit one or more of the above categories. It is our opinion that their clinical successes are seldom on a par with their media success. It is our opinion that humility and a non-dogmatic and accepting attitude in the clinician establishes a more productive therapeutic environment than power-seeking and arrogance. Better that these power drives are spent in building a professional organization to forward one's ideas, not acted out on those who came for treatment and not to be proselytized or used for the therapist's advantage.

THE STEREOTYPES OF THERAPISTS: ORIGIN AND FUNCTION

The therapist as imperious and power-seeking is not, to our knowledge, a common view of mental health professionals among the lay public. There are, however, several well-known stereotypes of psychotherapists that usually appear in novels, films, jokes, cartoons, and the mass media. These gross characterizations are of importance. Not only do they influence the public's (and hence our patient's) perceptions of us, but they also color our own view of ourselves and other professionals.

The classic stereotype is that of the Freudian psychoanalyst: a middle-aged man with a stern fatherly demeanor, Jewish, bearded, German accent, foreign born and trained, and usually a psychiatrist, as opposed to another mental health professional. In short, the typical German or Austrian psychiatrist of the 1930s, 1940s, and 1950s. Many of the first practitioners of modern dynamic psychotherapy in this country displayed these traits of the emigre analyst. Even today, there are many individuals who, without a personal experience with a psychotherapist, would probably respond with this image if asked to describe their idea of an analyst. This is especially true if the characterization is in a humorous vein. Think, for instance, whether you have ever seen a cartoon, film comedy, or read a joke, satire, or comic novel that did not portray the psychiatrist or other therapist in this stereotyped fashion.

It is significant that the classic character of the psychoanalyst is so often given the role of either a kooky, bumbling quack or that of a vaguely menacing, self-absorbed, and introverted scientist. This stereotype shares many attributes with that of the "mad scientist," another seriocomic figure. What then is the origin and function of this view? Partly it relates to certain realities (some psychoanalysts do fit this description) and partly to the mechanisms of myth making. Certainly not all therapists conform to this hackneyed model. Psychoanalytic concepts, however, have had a profound effect on the public consciousness in America. Freud's ideas brought to light both the phenomenon of the unconscious mind and the pervasive influence of repressed sexuality. Neither of these notions has tended to sooth or comfort many people. Acknowledging and exploring these psychoanalytic concepts was both fascinating in others and terrifying in oneself. We believe that the function of this stereotype, then, was to clearly label psychoanalysis as serious and worthy of attention, but also as something that related for the most part to outsiders and foreigners—people who were strange and "different from us." In doing so, a certain protection is assured and validated between the holders of the prejudgement.

As time went on, the number of foreign clinicians declined, and a substitute had to be found. Although this stereotype of the "psychoanalyst" continued as the humorous representation of the psychotherapist, a newer, more "American" character emerged. This character drew more on our romanticized vision of the physician in this country. He or she was not like other people. The physician was somehow more nobly endowed with intelligence, judgement, skill, and ability than the rest of us and possessed the mantle of "healer." We call this stereotype the "doctor." In many aspects it is more positive than the "analyst," the negative aspect being much more subtle. What this character lacks is humanness. The "analyst" had, at least, the luxury of personal idiosyncracies; he or she was allowed to be different. The "doctor," however, is basically a technician. He applies procedures to effect cures; his wisdom and knowledge is vast and invariably appropriate. His only failures are with stubborn patients who "refuse to be helped" or who are "beyond hope." This character embodies the American myth of science: the "doctor" knows all or will shortly know all— only more time and money are necessary. Unfortunately, while we can see through and laugh at the stereotype of the "analyst" not so many of us can do the same with the "doctor." The reader might consider how much he models, consciously or unconsciously, himself on this character.

The function of the "doctor" stereotype is more complex. While the "analyst" served primarily to separate the layman from his anxiety about the mysteries and threat of unconscious motivation, the "doctor" served primarily as a protective device for both professional and public. The clinician can invoke the "doctor" image to hide the woeful inadequacy of the tools of psychotherapy both from himself and from his patients. With the exception of the sometimes controversial, if often justified,

expedients of psychopharmacology and behavioral conditioning, we have few scientific tools as therapists. The medium of
treatment still remains our judgments in choosing the appropriate response to an individual patient. The skills we have obtained on interaction lie just as much within the realm of the
artisan as the technician. Diagnostic categories and specific
treatment procedures are certainly of great importance, but, in
our view, the therapist's relationship with the individual patient
is of equal, if not greater, significance.

Our overriding emphasis is to examine the role we assume
as people and professionals. It is not easy to confront these
issues, but psychotherapeutic work calls upon us to ask difficult
questions of others. Why should we be exempt?

Another common stereotype of psychotherapists is that
they are "crazier" than their patients. The origin of this viewpoint, like that of the analyst is two-fold. First, some therapists
are disturbed and have displayed this to others. Second, many
people would prefer that all therapists were crazy since this
belief would relieve them of their anxiety about the state of their
own sanity. This projective device serves a function for the
patient or prospective patient: since all "shrinks" are crazy,
there is no point in seeing one because they won't be able to help
you anyway.

The popular notion that therapists are "eccentric," "wild,"
or "crazy" also stems from their behavior which appears to be
generally more spontaneous, assertive, outspoken, and candid
when compared to most people's. Because of the therapist's
training and need to understand, fulfill himself, and live an
authentic life, the authors believe that most psychotherapists,
as a group, act, or attempt to act, more honestly than others.
Our society tends to be made uneasy and threatened by a display of genuine emotions. People are not accustomed to behavior that is not tinged with hypocrisy and superficiality. Thus,
psychotherapists, or for that matter any individual or group,
who strive to express themselves openly and honestly (or "hang
loose"), become "weird" or "crazy" in the public's mind.

The most positive stereotype of the psychotherapist consists of the kindly, strong, giving, patient, and wise parent figure. It also draws from the mythology of the physician. Instead of the more current "medical scientist" image, however, it seems closer to the old version of the country doctor who used to make house calls in the snow in the middle of the night. Although he might not have any medical miracles up his sleeve, he always gave his utmost as a human being. His bedside manner was as important to the healing process as his technical skills and his patients felt truly cared for. The parallels cannot be stretched too far here, but they seem important to the idea of the therapist.

The origin of this stereotype lies both in the image of the country doctor and in the needs, both symbolic and actual, of most patients for a positive and corrective parenting experience. Much of what constitutes effective psychotherapy relates to corrective emotional experiences with the therapist. The function of this stereotype can be positive and negative. It can, on one hand, serve as a mechanism that reflects an ideal which the therapist can never fulfill. The clinician is therefore rendered ineffective by this comparison. On the other hand, the positive function will mobilize the patient to relate to the clinician as an idealized parent-figure who will truly understand and help. Of all the conventional views of practitioners already considered, this one does the most to promote a productive attitude in both patient and therapist. It should only be remembered that kindness must always be tempered with practical realism. It is not enough to be merely concerned. As Heinlein (1961, p. 393) wrote: "Goodness is not enough. Without solid, hard wisdom, goodness alone cannot accomplish good."

The final stereotype, which is probably the most recent, originates from the new, radical therapeutic approaches that have grown out of the human potential/sensory awareness movements. For want of a better or more accepted term, we will call this the "far-out therapist." This therapist is found among the more controversial methods of what is basically a form of psychotherapy: encounter groups, sensory awareness groups, primal therapy, nude psychotherapy, psychedelic agents, meditation and other aspects of esoteric Eastern religious rituals, therapies utilizing the movement and manipulation of the body like Rolfing, and so on. The list of new approaches is endless. In addition, there are many techniques which were considered "far-out," or not within the mainstream of psychotherapeutic practice, several years ago, but which have become well established and accepted: Gestalt therapy, existential psychotherapy, psychodrama, dance, music, poetry, and art therapy, transactional analysis, rational-emotive therapy.

Again, the function of the stereotype is protective. The process of labeling an idea as strange, misguided, ridiculous, and dangerous serves to direct negative attention towards the innovator. It is not always a matter of those who are stereotyping being threatened with a loss of status, position, or financial security to the newcomers. Most of us are disconcerted by the thought of change and leaving the security of an old idea. Often we will label and oppose innovation because it speaks so strongly to those needs we have denied. All these "far-out" therapies appeal to strong inner needs. If this were not so, no one would have been interested enough to support their proliferation and growing acceptance. How many readers, for instance, are not intrigued by the idea of participating (or perhaps, more safely, observing) a nude marathon group, a session under the influence of LSD, or being Rolfed (a massage technique)? How many who have not experienced it personally have wondered whether there was anything to meditation, transpersonal states, or an encounter group?

We have considered some of the common stereotypes of psychotherapists and psychotherapy along with some of their probable origins and function. As outlined, these stereotypes are based on a distortion of some real or observable quality of the treatment process and the participants as it relates positively or negatively to the social realities of the observers. The function of stereotyping usually involves (1) either a protective, self-distancing from some threatening aspect of the therapy, or (2) some dependency that stems from a need to identify with the therapist. Not only do these stereotypes have a powerful and pervasive effect on the patient and public, but also on the attitudes and values of psychotherapists. How we, as professionals, perceive ourselves may be strongly grounded on the kinds of role-identifications that underlie these stereotypes. This self-perception will influence our everyday clinical judgments and reactions to our patients. Every psychotherapist should be ever aware of this tendency, and try to discard the "safe" delusion that stereotyping is something that other people do. You do it and so do we.

What It's Like to Be a Therapist

Those readers who have not yet begun to practice have, no doubt, wondered what it is like to be a psychotherapist. What is it like to fulfill a social role that involves so much mystery, tragedy, and responsibility? This, again, is an area that evokes stereotyped thinking in most people who have not yet experienced practicing therapy. The authors would like to address this phenomenon from their own experiences.

Being Responsible for Others

Every psychotherapist has often been asked by friends and acquaintances: "What is it like?" In the abstract, this is a difficult question to answer. Frequently, only the most standard cliches come to mind: challenging, rewarding to help people, good to work for yourself (for those in private practice), never boring, and so on. The experience can be hard to express and define without referring to specific individuals and cases, which is a taboo. As a result, therapists usually seem enigmatic about their work, a reaction that both grows from and feeds the mystique of being a psychotherapist. Actually, there is nothing particularly mysterious or esoteric about much of what a therapist does. Fundamentally, therapists talk to people about their problems. We are a "special friend" to those we treat, someone separate from their ordinary sphere of living who has had specific training in listening and understanding about the various ways in which people perceive and interact with themselves and others. Essentially, the therapist's task is to help people identify and clarify the sources and results of their misconceptions, to discover and devise corrective perceptions and actions to deal with what they conceive to be problems that impair effective and satisfying living.

An almost universal reaction among people about the practice of psychotherapy is some version of: "It must be a terrible strain to be responsible for all those people's lives," or "I could never be able to handle all that responsibility." This is related frequently with a curious mixture of envy (that therapists are so powerful) and relief (that they do not have to shoulder this burden). Although the authors have heard this reaction repeatedly, it still strikes a discordant note since this view is quite different from our own perception. Most often our reactions to these comments are some variant of: "It's true that patients often try to get us to assume that kind of responsibility." In fact, to take responsibility for anyone's life is more a part of the problem than the solution. An effective and competent therapist does not attempt to take on the burden of the patient's problems. It is more than enough to be responsible *for* oneself. We are only responsible *to* our patients.

Being Wise and All-Knowing

Another dilemma that awaits the therapist who escapes being responsible for his patients, is the expectation of being wise and omniscient. In a sense, one is a corollary of the other. Psychotherapists are the wise men, the secular clergy, if you will, of our culture. Both friend and patient will come to us with their dilemmas as some go to priests and oracles. Through our

mysterious power and secret knowledge about how human beings function, we are supposed to know what advice to give and
how to predict the future. Beware of the trap of trying to
portray the wise man, however strong the temptation. Although this phenomenon will occur most strongly with those
you treat, it may also be a factor in your personal relationships.
Remember that a therapist occupies a special position in the
eyes of others.

Frequently people will be uncomfortable in the company
of a psychotherapist, a "shrink." This unease, and its dynamics,
is probably related to the discomfort which is often felt in our
society when one is in the presence of the clergy (or similar
parent figures with powers of judgment). Many implicitly believe and expect that the clergy (omnipotent parents) are more
righteous and good-hearted, and that we must conceal our
"sinfulness" and inadequacies lest we be judged badly. Therapists produce similar reactions, although the quality of "sinfulness" takes a more secular character. Whereas, with the clergy,
we are aware of our spiritual and moral failings, with psychotherapists we are worried that our emotional difficulties and
shortcomings will be observed. "Badness" is transmuted into
"craziness." Fortunately, this is usually a transient phenomenon that lessens appreciably as the person gets to know us
better. Nevertheless, this tendency to feel uneasy in our presence always remains a factor on some level of interaction.

Being Isolated

Viewed as being "different" from other people, the psychotherapist is subjected to another common reaction from acquaintances and friends: the concern that you're going to
"psychoanalyze" them. Often stated in a joking manner, this
anxiety, however, is thinly disguised. The ubiquity of this reaction has led many therapists to be defensive about their work.
Others are reluctant to tell people what they do for a living. Still

others capitalize on this anxiety and speak of little else but psychotherapy, enjoying the opportunity to intimidate others. The latter is probably the most defensive position of all and ultimately the most isolating.

Since the therapist's work is fascinating and frightening to most individuals, an inherent occupational hazard is to isolate yourself from others, at least initially. Although the experienced therapist becomes accustomed to this phenomenon, it is wise to remind yourself periodically of this aspect of being a therapist. There is little that can be done about this isolation, per se, other than to understand it, accept it, and continue to be your natural self.

The danger of becoming too insulated and out of touch with colleagues and professional developments is another aspect of professional isolation. To avoid and combat this pitfall every therapist should endeavor to maintain professional contacts, either formal or informal, by attendance at regular professional associations and meetings, training workshops, or community involvement and consultant work. Without the stimulation and variety of professional experiences other than just psychotherapeutic practice, therapists are in danger of becoming cut-off from their own professional milieu and operating in a narrow vacuum. As a corollary, the authors further believe in and endorse the importance of developing active hobbies and interests, e.g., sports, theater, art, and music, that enable the therapist to broaden his interest in life and the people around him. If anyone should be a well-rounded person, actively engaged in life, we believe it should be the psychotherapist who must deal with and understand people of varying backgrounds and personalities.

Experience in living, to our mind, provides the best training ground for understanding and appreciating the infinite variety of the human condition. Consider for a moment how limited, experientially, the novice therapist is. Usually brought up in a middle class urban background, the therapist completes his education and training while in his middle or late twenties.

Now ready to begin practice, the beginning clinician has not only had a minimal exposure to a variety of life situations, but has also lived in a narrow frame of reference as a student struggling to compete successfully. Though this formulation sounds simplistic, it nevertheless has validity for many novice therapists. Our point is to be aware that your limited life experiences will influence, and even limit, your effectiveness as an emerging therapist. A much-admired professor of ours used to emphasize repeatedly that the best preparation for becoming a sensitive and effective clinician and psychotherapist is a lot of living. This professor confessed that his years as a cub reporter covering local crime and the usual sob stories gave him a knowledge and feeling for others that proved an invaluable foundation for his professional life. Similarly, one of the authors believes that his years of working as a bartender and service in the U.S. Army were experiences equally valuable in providing a sense of the breadth of life. Incidentally, as one grows and develops as a person, the psychotherapist builds up a repertoire of experiences and life situations which can be recalled to provide a deeper understanding and appreciation of a particular patient's problem.

On Not Being a Person

As prospective clinicians you should begin to be prepared for a rather unpleasant reality: those you treat will seldom see and relate to you as a whole human being. Rather, you will be a semi-deified, idealized figure. Less frequently, you will also personify all that is judgmental, negative, and rejecting in their experience. There will be occasions where mistakes on the part of the therapist will contribute to and exacerbate these distortions. For the most part, however, distortions will occur regardless of whether we are doing the right or the wrong thing, technically speaking.

A certain sadness and loneliness accompanies this reality. Psychotherapists are only human beings after all, and the time we spend with patients makes up a large, perhaps the single largest, portion of our interaction with others. There is both an irony and a dilemma herein. The irony is that while we are charged with helping patients relate more freely and constructively with themselves and others, we must do so in a setting where the therapist receives little, if any, real, positive, interpersonal feedback or satisfaction. The dilemma resides in the necessity of maintaining the ability to provide an emotionally open and accepting environment without receiving the same reenforcement from the patient. The rewards from our calling are essentially indirect, and our motivation, by necessity, internal and self-validating. It is difficult work; it denies and is oblivious to our immediate emotional needs. As a result, the practice of psychotherapy calls for a high degree of personal security, dedication, and the ability to obtain gratification from an interpersonal relationship that may not always be characterized by clear and dramatic therapeutic success.

Thus far, it may have crossed the reader's mind that we seem to be dwelling on rather subtle, philosophical issues. It is quite possible, in fact, to practice psychotherapy without ever directly considering many of these aspects. The authors are aware of this and are stressing these issues for several reasons: 1) they are important to our conception of therapy as an interpersonal process in which the therapist's internal process is of prime importance; 2) they are often overlooked in the more technically oriented writings on psychotherapy; 3) in the authors' supervisory experience, these issues came up again and again as a meaningful part of the difficulties faced in beginning practice; and 4) they are so clearly in tune with our own personal experience in clinical practice.

WHAT MAKES AN EFFECTIVE THERAPIST?

The authors' conception of the personal and professional characteristics of an effective psychotherapist relates directly to the implications of the issues already discussed in this chapter. In addition, several other attributes will be enumerated. This list is not meant to exhaust all possibilities; nor should it be considered as an absolute statement since some of the issues and attributes are more flexible than others. We are aware that it is possible for an effective therapist to differ substantially from our notions. These ideas are meant as guidelines and as stimuli for thought. Whether or not you, the reader, fit or do not fit one or more of these categories is not the point. It is our intention to raise these issues as a point of view which will help stimulate your thoughts and reactions.

Wanting to be a Therapist

One should choose to engage in psychotherapy primarily for its own sake, not as an expedient, or as a path to some other goal, like power, prestige, or financial security. More important, this choice must be reaffirmed continually. A therapist must enjoy the work and not merely continue in it because other options appear closed or too difficult to change into "after all the training I've been through."

Well Trained

Adequate preparation to do effective psychotherapy requires many years of training. It is doubtful that any clinician will even begin to feel comfortable and competent until he has had at least several years of direct clinical experience. The particular mode of preparation (formal academic, internship, training institute, etc.) is not nearly as important as the presence of adequate and competent supervision. Training must include both the cognitive aspects (to provide a theoretical structure) and the experiential (to provide a direct, effective involvement and understanding). The specific theoretical school or treatment modalities utilized are relevant only in that they must be compatible with the personal character structure and style of the individual practitioner and conform to basic ethical standards.

Personal Life

If the personal life of a therapist is not reasonably in order or progressing meaningfully in that direction, it will have a direct, negative influence on his or her clinical effectiveness. This is not to deny that psychotherapists are human and have their problems. What we do not have, however, is the luxury of allowing our difficulties to go undealt with. "Physician! heal thyself" is a maxim that should be ever kept in mind when evaluating our own problems. The therapist should be aware of his intrapersonal conflicts and motivations and attempt to clarify and deal with them. This attempt at clarification and understanding is an ongoing process, not a one-time affair. For this reason, personal therapy is viewed as a necessary part of professional training. Moreover, a continuing self-examination is also indispensable. The training of a capable therapist is never really complete. None of us knows everything there is to know. And few of us know as much as we should.

Humility, Power, and Responsibility

Any therapist who hopes to be effective must develop and possess a profound sense of humility about his own strengths and weaknesses as a healing agent. The therapist's power lies in assisting change, not causing it to happen. If these needs for power are not firmly in hand there will be a strong tendency to shift emphasis from helping to change, to forcing or manipulating change. At this point, a therapist crosses an ethical and professional Rubicon from which it is usually difficult to return, with potentially disastrous consequences for both practitioner and client. Understanding this, the therapist will be clear as to his responsibility. We are responsible *to* our client, never *for* them.

Understanding Roles and Stereotypes

The skilled therapist has examined and developed an understanding of and made a personal peace with his attitudes towards the various social role behaviors and stereotypes, which were discussed earlier, that relate to psychotherapy. The clinician must be cognizant of the stereotypes already mentioned if he is to avoid being a mere technician who reacts with whatever styles or role expectations are popular at the moment. Being one's self is not as simple a process as it first appears. First, one must know one's own role.

Character and Personality Traits

There are a number of character and personality traits that the authors believe are related to effectiveness in psychotherapists. We do not mean that only individuals who naturally and spontaneously exhibit this constellation of behaviors can be skillful and successful clinicians. Quite the contrary, all of these characteristics fall within the normal and usual spectrum of behavior. For some individuals it might require a toning down of their natural gregariousness; for others, learning to extend themselves somewhat beyond their usual limits. Being a competent therapist involves mastering a number of deceptively simple skills. The reader may be tempted, here again, to dismiss some or all of the following as being obvious and simplistic. Yet, we have found and believe that most of the difficulties that beginning therapists exhibit are related directly to weaknesses in the following basic personal qualities of behavior and communication. Novice practitioners must learn to control their tendency to look for the complicated and esoteric both in diagnosing the patient's difficulty and in analyzing their own errors and blocks to effective work. They should begin with the basics. Our elaborations are only as sturdy as the foundation they are built upon.

1) BE INTERESTED.   That the therapist convey a convincing sense of being interested is of crucial importance in relating to any patient. It is irrelevant to the patient whether or not you are really interested if you do not effectively communicate that his problem is important to you. This attention must be sincere.

2) BE INTERESTING.   The complement of being interested is being interesting. Boring therapists have dull sessions and blunt their patients' ability to communicate or relate. Psychotherapy resembles, in many ways, a social interaction with social role expectations operating on both sides. The therapist must expect and accept constricted affect or evasiveness on the part of the client, but it cannot be accepted in the therapist. An older colleague once remarked that every good clinician is also a good actor. We believe this to be true. Not in the sense of make-believe or being untrue, but that whatever is discussed is projected with appropriate force, meaning, and conviction to the other participant in the interaction.

3) BE ACTIVE OR PASSIVE.   As already noted, the authors hold that (as distinct from orthodox psychoanalysis) the clinician who participates actively in the therapeutic process is more successful than the passive therapist. Being passive and affectless obscures the person of the therapist from the patient. In order to build a therapeutic alliance as quickly as possible, we should begin to actively solicit cooperation from those we treat. It is neither appropriate nor economical to merely sit back and wait for a working alliance to occur.

4) BE OUTGOING.   One of the primary tasks of treatment is to secure information. Patients are often fearful and reluctant to disclose painful and distressing material which could inhibit their interaction with you. To counter this, the therapist should present an outgoing demeanor that actively demonstrates his accessability and readiness to listen and understand. This outgoing demeanor is both conscious and controlled. Some clini-

cians may find it necessary to put a rein on their usual tendency to verbally dominate the interaction. The focus, after all, is the patient's productions, not the therapist's. Still others will need to combat their usual proclivity to remain quiet as this will tend to inhibit communication. A balance must be struck.

5) BE EMPATHIC AND COMPASSIONATE. Empathy denotes "the capacity for participation in another's feelings or ideas" (Webster Dictionary 1977); the German Ein-fühlung, translated as "a feeling-in," best gives the flavor of empathy. Perhaps the most pervasive fear in the minds of patients is that others will not be able to understand and accept their thoughts, feelings, and experiences. Clinicians must be able to convey convincingly their ability to sympathize with those they treat.

Equally difficult to define is the quality of compassion which may not be too different from empathy. The authors view compassion in terms similar to Rubin's (1975), as both the opposition and the antidote for the self-hate that is so characteristic of those we see as patients. Compassion is defined as a "feeling for another's sorrow or hardship that leads to help" (Rubin 1975, p. 31). This is almost a definition of psychotherapy, since without the "feeling for," the process becomes a technical exercise, and without the "help," it is merely idle and disconnected pity or sympathy.

6) BE NONDEFENSIVE AND OPEN. It seems ludicrous to state that a psychotherapist should be nondefensive, and yet the obvious must be stated. This is especially true for the beginning practitioner who is usually less than comfortable with his command of the discipline. You will be challenged often by patients, both directly and indirectly. How to deal with these challenges is a series of continuing choices. Often your own feelings of personal or professional inadequacy will tempt you to retreat behind the too-handy facade of technique and clinical distance. The best "defense," however, is a willingness to accept and acknowledge, at least to one's self, the inevitability of these

reactions. This is part of the learning process we all go through. The proficient therapist can honestly look at and examine his personal reactions to the therapeutic encounter. Such openness proceeds from a realistic assessment of his responsibilities and limitations. This is the therapist who can acknowledge his strengths and weaknesses as a human being and professional without feeling obliged to defend what he does not believe or know about.

7) SELF-DISCLOSURE.   Closely related to the idea of being open is the issue of self-disclosure. All therapists will frequently be asked by patients for information about themselves. These requests are often reasonable and legitimate and can be responded to simply and directly, except in circumstances that reflect testing, manipulating, or evading the therapist. Besides, there will be occasions when some behavior or experience in the patient's life will strike the therapist as being quite similar to some experience of his own. At these times it may be often helpful and appropriate to mention your experiences with a brief discussion of the similarities and differences. Self-disclosure can be a most beneficial aspect of therapeutic interaction if the technique is not used to impress or secure sympathy from the patient. Used appropriately, it tends to help close the gap between client and therapist, reenforce their mutual humanness, and strengthen the alliance. Like all powerful and effective techniques, however, it must be used with discretion and careful observation of the patient's reaction. The concept of self-disclosure with examples will be further outlined in Chapter 5.

8) BE ECONOMICAL AND THINK CLEARLY.   Novice as well as experienced practitioners must learn to recognize and control a tendency to look for the complicated and esoteric when diagnosing and treating the patient. This tendency to overanalyze also operates when the therapist looks to himself to understand his own countertransference and errors of technique that hinder effective therapy. Follow science's law of parsimony and formu-

late ideas in clear, simple terms with the utmost economy of explanation. This mode of thought may be labeled pejoratively by some as relying too much on common sense. Yet, we feel that using one's common sense in combination with one's technical skills is an uncommon and invaluable approach in understanding human behavior.

The authors realize that successful psychotherapists are not a "type," and that they include a broad spectrum of personality characteristics and styles. Each clinician brings to the therapeutic encounter his own idiosyncratic point of view and responses which reflect his own biases. As a result, no two therapists will handle a given situation in exactly the same way. The foregoing behavioral characteristics, which we believe contribute greatly to therapeutic skill and efficacy, are not the last word in therapeutic technique. The authors do not presume to adopt a rigid position in this regard since many roads lead to therapeutic expertise. In our experience, however, therapists whom we have admired and found most successful and competent were those who most closely approximated the personality style and traits discussed above.

THE EFFECTS OF BEING A THERAPIST

The final issue that needs to be raised concerns how the practice of psychotherapy affects the therapist's own emotional life and thoughts. To be a psychotherapist is to be confronted daily with conflict, avoidance, hypocrisy, dishonesty, aggression, and self-hate. These things are a part of everyone's daily experience, but therapists deal with them more directly and purposively. Patients display these characteristics because they have yet to find a viable method for resolving their searing conflicts, and not because they are more evil or perverse than anyone else. Patients are in conflict about what they want to do when it apparently opposes what they seem allowed to do. The therapist, as a human being socialized in the same cultural milieu, inevitably experiences many similar difficulties. What then is the effect of being reminded every day in one's work of these dilemmas? This factor probably explains the frequent comment among laymen who "don't see how we could listen to that stuff day after day without getting depressed or crazy ourselves." Although a good point, it is seldom discussed in professional literature. Performing psychotherapy, at times, can be a brutalizing and wearying experience. This is especially true when (1) the clinician is overworked or has inadequate control over the many important variables of the treatment setting, e.g., practicing in a poorly administered and/or under-staffed institutional milieu or overloaded community clinic; (2) the novice therapist is improperly trained and supervised, and given insufficient support. Finally, it can be true even for experienced clinicians who have not attained an understanding of their role and responsibilities, and who have not achieved a working alliance with their own neurotic conflicts.

Practicing psychotherapy can, and should be, however, a growth experience for the therapist as well as the patient. An oft-repeated truism in education states that the teacher often learns more than the students. In a similar vein, the same holds for psychotherapy, which is, after all, also an educative experience. Colleagues have often commented that being a therapist helps to "keep them honest"—honest with themselves and with others. And well it should—we, as clinicians, are exposed daily to the intra- and interpersonal difficulties of our clients. Exposed daily to the stresses and crises of patients, the therapist cannot avoid seeing the parallels between the irrational behavior of his patients and his own conflicted past or present behavior patterns. Those we work with are not always so dissimilar from ourselves.

Being able then to see the pathology or disturbance, are we not trained to be aware of the prophylaxis? And if we see in the difficulties of patients a mirror of our own problems, should we not also know what can and should be done in our own lives? Is not, in fact, the observation of these phenomena in others a reminder of whatever unfinished business remains in our own growth and development as a person? The authors have found this to be true and, indirectly, a blessing of psychotherapeutic work. How, indeed, can we confront a patient about his difficulties if we, the therapists, are not also making the necessary efforts to remedy such problems in our own lives.

In a sense, this is one of the fringe benefits of the job; a gentle (or not so gentle) daily reminder of matters that need attending to; a reminder that can be of immeasurable help to the therapist and promote his personal growth. But, reminders can also be avoided. As with patients who often know better ways of coping and yet continue to choose not to enact them, so can we rationalize our own avoidance. This avoidance, however, can only be engaged in at one's personal and professional peril. It is not that we must be perfect paragons of emotional health, but we *must* be engaged and evolving as human beings. If not, what we say and what we do becomes dishonest, and dishonesty is incompatible with the work we do. Thus, we create a separation and emotional detachment that cannot fail to compromise our efficacy. One can never be perfectly grown, but one can be continually growing. Use this opportunity wisely: those we assist can also be of assistance to us.

Unquestionably the greatest effect of practicing therapy is the enormous sense of challenge, excitement, enjoyment, and personal gratification that every therapist experiences from working with patients. Using one's skills, knowledge, and creativity in the service of helping another human being represents to us the epitome of achieving self-fulfillment and a oneness with Everyman. Our beliefs are best exemplified by the therapist who, during a recent supervisory session, glowed with pride and happiness as she described the patient's emerging growth, and suddenly exclaimed, "I should be paying for this experience rather than the patient." As experienced therapists, the authors still find it surprising to be paid for work which provides such great enjoyment and satisfaction. Naive sentiments? Perhaps. But sentiments that need to be clearly felt and expressed if one is a therapist. For without such emotions and reactions to the practice of psychotherapy, you, the psychotherapist, have chosen the wrong profession. Practicing psychotherapy requires and means, if anything, an emotional commitment to the patient. Therefore, if you cannot experience, or rarely feel, excitement and satisfaction from practicing psychotherapy, you will be hard put to make the emotional investment in the patient that is required of our profession.

Chapter 4

THE INITIAL CONSULTATION

The first interview with a patient is a time of anxiety and uncertainty for both the therapist and the patient. Each realizes, consciously or not, that some degree of trust and positive feeling must be established; that a connection with someone else must be made in order to begin a dialogue. As therapists, we need to project an aura of confidence, strength, and interest in what is troubling the patient. We want the person to like and feel safe with us; we also want to like the person. Positive rapport may not be readily established, however, because of the patient's severe anxiety, anger, and distrust, and/or the therapist's own discomfort. Whatever the reasons, and many may exist on both sides, the therapist must be aware of any lack of effective communication and rapport, and proceed accordingly. He should react in a fashion that is minimally threatening to the patient, and that shows an eagerness to listen to the problem being presented. At the same time, the therapist should be evaluating the emotional climate as it falls short of being comfortable or positive. Knowing the factors that interfere with good rapport is necessary if we are to gain a quicker appreciation of the patient's needs.

The form and content of these initial sessions will vary considerably from patient to patient depending upon the therapist's assessment of the individual's emotional state at the time of the interview. The clinician should have in mind a general outline of the kind of information he wishes to obtain. Securing this cannot take precedence over responding to the immediate needs of the patient. With most beginning sessions, obtaining background data should proceed without difficulty. The therapist must, however, be always on the alert for signals that indicate when a digression is called for. During a recent initial session, for example, the therapist suddenly became aware of a patient's insatiable need for attention and readiness to feel rejected when he complained, to our consternation, that questions were too perfunctory and academic, and did not allow for him to talk as freely as he would like. Following this cue and slowing down the tempo of the questions, the therapist responded more to the patient's need to discuss his professional life as a musician. Upon showing a stronger interest in the patient's professional life, which represented the focal point of his existence, he became more friendly, candid, and less guarded. In this first meeting, the therapist must be constantly aware of the patient's feelings in order to maximize, as much as possible, a positive emotional climate. Obtaining background information and eliciting personal reactions can then proceed smoothly.

GOALS OF THE INITIAL INTERVIEW

The major goal of the initial consultation is to obtain information and to arrive at an initial assessment of the problems. Specifically, the therapist should determine:

1. who referred the patient and why
2. the nature of the presenting complaints
3. the patient's background, or a brief case history

The therapist should, therefore, explain that during this first meeting he needs to understand why the patient is seeking therapy and how he views his problems. Further, that you will ask many questions to obtain a picture of his background. Let the patient know immediately, as you are writing down the usual identifying data, that you will be making some written notes of his remarks, and that at the end of the session you will summarize your impression of the problem, and outline the next steps. Either during these opening remarks, or during the summarizing statement, indicate how many separate sessions (the authors usually require three sessions) will be needed to complete the evaluation or diagnostic consultation phase. It is helpful to explain that these sessions will provide more detailed information, enable some diagnostic psychological testing (if you use them) and conclude with your diagnostic impression and recommendations, as well as an explanation of psychotherapy, if indicated.

At the close of this first session the therapist should discuss fees noting that there is no obligation to continue in therapy with you, but that you will take responsibility to make a referral to a more appropriate resource, if desired. Stress is placed on the fact that limited finances need not prevent one from receiving mental health services that are available for nominal fees in community clinics. This is an important issue since finances can discourage many individuals from seeking or continuing therapy. The rationale behind the initial consultation is to provide the patient with a structure that makes the interview a meaningful experience. By proceeding in a structured manner, the initial consultation will serve to turn the interview from a confusing and anxious encounter into a clarifying, reassuring, and informative experience. It will then help establish a give-and-take between the therapist and patient that allows the beginning relationship, as the musician says of a performance, to "breathe," and follow a natural rhythm. As a guiding rule, this consultation phase should be geared toward providing a useful and beneficial experience, even though the patient chooses not to continue.

REASON FOR REFERRAL

A consideration of the specifics of the initial consultation is now in order. First, it is important to know who referred the patient, and why the patient was referred to you. Did the patient come on his own, or was he forced or encouraged to come by a parent, mate, or friend? The answer to this question provides some idea of the patient's motivation and the influences that affect his decisions. Is the patient placating or submitting to someone else because the relationship with that person is deteriorating, or is he responding maturely to someone else's concern? The latter would be suggestive of an emerging degree of insight and/or an ability to tolerate criticism. Furthermore, is the referring person a former patient or someone known to the therapist, a factor that would influence how the patient views you. For example, a former patient once referred a friend who expressed confidence that he could be helped because the therapist was successful in helping the friend with a similar marital problem. In this situation, we were fortunate to begin therapy with an individual who had built-in confidence and an optimistic outlook for being helped. On the other hand, patients like teenagers and young adults who are pressured by their parents can present all kinds of subtle and overt resistances that must be acknowledged and understood by the therapist.

A 16-year-old boy, Tom, was brought for a consultation by his father who was concerned with his son's failing grades, withdrawal, and lack of communication since the mother's death two years ago. We learned that Tom, despite his passive resistance, was desperately seeking a substitute parent relationship under the guise of wanting to develop his self-confidence. Submitting to his father's demand to obtain therapy represented Tom's way of receiving more of the father's attention. Therapy meant that the father had to leave work early and drive Tom to his appointment. Thus, Tom gained attention from a father who otherwise spent little time at home. This knowledge quickly made the therapist aware of Tom's intense feeling of deprivation and enormous need for love and attention, and the basis for motivating Tom into therapy.

Individuals who are self-referred generally sustain a high degree of self-determination and motivation. They come to therapy because of inner-directed pressures and are therefore not trying to be pleasing by submitting to someone else. An example of how a person may seek therapy as a result of self-motivation and external pressures is the case of Don, a 40-year-old who could no longer control the anger toward his wife and was fearful that he would physically attack her. His wife, who was becoming increasingly upset about his temper outbursts toward her and their four daughters, reinforced Don's desire to obtain counseling. But Don interpreted his wife's demand that he seek therapy as another instance of her rejection. Consequently, he began resisting therapy after several sessions as a way to attack her. This illustrates the many subtle nuances that prevail to bring a person into therapy. Clarifying and understanding the forces that brought the patient to you is the first step in developing a grasp of the individual's dynamics.

THE PRESENTING COMPLAINT

After establishing how the person was referred, he should be asked to describe his chief complaints and the precipitating factor(s) that brought him for help. Immediately determining how he came for therapy and the presenting problem quickly structures the interview and provides a focus for further questions. Obtaining a precise and detailed description of the patient's presenting symptoms is of utmost importance in understanding his major anxieties, stresses, and distortions. It is a truism that communication, i.e., language, may become distorted by our own needs. Therefore, whatever a patient reports as the problem (depressive moods, or feelings of inadequacy, or aggressive behavior, etc.), the therapist should ask him to explain in detail, with concrete examples and in different words, what he means and how he views his complaint. The person's definition of a symptom may differ radically from your understanding of a specific term. For example, the patient may use the word "depression" to describe emotions and behavior that, upon questioning, describe reactions that differ from the clinical view of depression. An effective way to clarify communication is by asking the patient to describe the different situations in which the symptom occurs, and to describe the symptom with synonyms ("What other words would you use?" or "how else would you describe this feeling, or problem?").

This approach, simple as it sounds, can provide a surprising amount of information. So often we incorrectly assume that we know what another person means, especially when cliches like "anger," "guilt," "depression," "anxiety," are used. Prodding the patient to "say it differently" and describe the situation in depth will bring forth a clearer understanding of the emotion, and may expose underlying dynamics. In our pseudo-psychologically sophisticated culture, the therapist must be especially careful to define cliche-ridden phrases.

Situational and time elements are other factors that further refine your understanding of the presenting complaint. Under what circumstances does the symptom occur? What was the situation when Don was bombarded with feelings of hatred and aggressive impulses toward his wife? The answer, in that case, ranged widely from situations in which his wife 1) arrives at a decision that the house needs the attic remodeled, 2) frowns upon his taking an extra drink, 3) asks him to be easier on the children, 4) criticizes him for his growing flabbiness, and 5) expresses a desire to return to work when the children are older. These illustrations from Don suggest 1) a deeply ingrained resentment toward his wife, who presents 2) a threat to his ego, which 3) needs to be in control much of the time.

Questioning the patient to determine when the symptom first appeared, and the frequency of occurence, provides an idea of its intensity and pervasiveness. Also, learning whether the symptom, or similar behavior, ever occurred in the patient's past offers another clue to underlying dynamics. Don's responses revealed that aggressive reactions toward his wife increased in frequency since he was passed over for a job promotion eight years ago. Besides, he remembered flashes of similar hostility during his teenage years whenever his mother worked overtime and could not prepare dinner for him, or take care of his everyday needs. These revelations pointed up the profound and deeply-rooted nature of Don's hostility toward female figures. To Don, females were viewed as depriving and rejecting. The anger aroused by Don's disappointments became displaced onto his wife whom he blamed for all his present problems. These examples show how close and precise questioning of the situations and time period during which the symptom occurred can lead to significant tentative formulations of the patient's dynamics.

OBTAINING THE PATIENT'S HISTORY

Emphasis on focus and structure is one of the major themes of this text. Nowhere is this more important than during the initial meeting with the patient, and especially when taking the case history. Time and time again, experience has shown that a well-detailed case history can provide information that is crucial in differential diagnosis, and in developing appropriate therapeutic plans. Some therapists may resist obtaining background material under the mistaken notion that this interferes with the natural therapeutic interaction. The patient may also resist providing historical information and prefer to focus on immediate problems rather than the past. Besides, much of this material we seek usually evokes negative emotions in the patient. Consequently, patients may prefer not to remember past events, especially of a detailed nature. Here again the therapist must maintain focus and gently insist on securing this case history material, yet remaining aware of the patient's reactions.

The following comprise the major topics that should be covered in the case history:

1. Chief complaints and presenting symptoms
2. Physical condition
3. Education
4. Social relationships
5. Sexual relationships
6. Vocational adjustment
7. Family relationships
8. Marital relations
9. Interests and hobbies

Each of these areas will be briefly touched upon with a view toward suggesting major points of emphasis.

Chief Complaints and Presenting Symptoms

The type of information to be obtained was discussed above.

Physical Condition

This comprises a list of the patient's important illnesses or injuries, physical complaints and concerns. Psychotherapy should never proceed until the therapist has a clear understanding of the nature and effects of a medical problem for which the individual has or is now receiving medical treatment. Knowing the extent of a patient's physical illness, information which may require speaking to the treating physician, may enable the therapist to grasp the significance of the psychological symptoms. The type of physical complaints presented will also suggest how the patient views himself through bodily awareness, indicative of the degree of hypochondriacal thinking and susceptibility to psychosomatic reactions. Learning that a patient suffers from a chronic lower back pain, which has never been helped by medical treatment and causes fatigue and fear of physical activity, will allow the therapist to appreciate the patient's symptoms of anxiety, depression, and sense of helplessness when they occur during periods of back pain. Furthermore, this symptom of back pain may hint at ways the patient reacts to emotional stress.

Education

The amount of formal and informal education completed, grades, attitudes toward learning, and reactions toward teachers indicate the patient's mental ability and level of intellectual functioning, as well as attitudes toward authority. Educational information will also tell much about the patient's ability to persevere, attitude toward "success," and manner of dealing with authority.

Social Relationships

To socialize, to be a part of someone else, to interact with others, is one of the most basic of all human needs. The manner in which a person relates to others and the degree to which he allows personal involvement and intimacy reveal much about the individual.

How many and what kind of friends does the patient have? What type of social activities are pursued? Is the patient a leader or follower? What problems exist in socializing with men and women? How is the patient viewed by others? The answers to these basic questions will reveal a great deal about the adequacy of social skills, attitudes towards others, and ideas of self-worth. The key concepts are self-worth, social skills, acceptance of others, empathy, and sharing. Most, if not all, of the conflicts reported by patients will manifest themselves in their social relationships.

Sexual Relationships

Sexuality is one of the most basic human needs and drives. The case history should obtain a thorough overview of the sexual experiences and attitudes of the patient. What were the early memories and experiences concerning sex? How did the patient feel about himself as a sexual being? When and under what circumstances did the first sexual activities occur? Has sexual intercourse been experienced? What were the initial thoughts and emotions to intercourse? What are the attitudes towards masturbation, orgasm, sexual play, age, and sexuality (including menopause), etc. How much and what kind of sex education was provided? Reactions to these questions will reflect the patient's attitudes and values about sexuality and the opposite sex, feelings of adequacy, anxiety about intimacy, and needs for affection as expressed through sexual contexts.

The emphasis placed upon sexuality in psychotherapy will differ from individual to individual and from therapist to therapist. Sex is an important part of the lives of all patients, either in its presence or absence. As therapists, we should be aware of our own attitudes and sensitive to the patient's attitudes so that we neither over- nor underemphasize this aspect in therapy.

Vocational Adjustment

Information regarding the patient's ambitions and ability to be independent, deal with authority, make plans, and cope with pressures can be inferred from his job history. Career goals and vocational outlook can add to your evaluation of the patient's motivation for achievement as well as his view of life, success, and reality testing. Inquiries to elicit this knowledge should focus on type and length of employment, job interests and goals, and relations with employers and co-workers. Unfortunately, therapists tend to neglect or minimize the patient's vocational adjustment and future career goals, and thereby overlook a rich source of information about the patient's functioning. Perhaps this minimal interest in the patient's vocational adjustment is associated with the professional's misguided notion that such information is not dynamic enough and too mundane for understanding personality functioning. Considering that work represents the way most individuals spend the majority of their waking hours, an understanding of the patient's job, vocational interests and goals will provide invaluable information on his life style and ego functioning.

Family Relationships

Probably the most important case history information available will concern the patient's relations to his parents and siblings. Parental values, attitudes, influences, and expectations will delineate the emotional atmosphere in which the patient was reared. The patient's feelings of security can be inferred from the degree of acceptance and love that was experienced from parents. Since asking people about their parents is usually a threatening question which can arouse immediate resistance and defensiveness, it is best initially to avoid questions that ask how a patient relates to or gets along with a parent. An effective and less threatening opening is: how would you describe your father, your mother? And then, how would you describe your relations with them? What are their expectations of you? Determining with which parent the patient most identifies and to whom he is closest, indicates much about the patient's sense of identity and significant parental influences.

Other effective questions for eliciting material about the patient's relations with parents are: What do you like most and least about each parent? In what way would you like to be like your father and mother?

Finally, a view of how the parents get along with each other offers a measure of the emotional climate in the home. Which parent makes the decisions, and how decisions are made provide material concerning family unity and the kind of respect and acceptance that exists among family members.

Knowledge of how the patient relates to siblings indicates the degree of rivalry, and whether siblings represent positive or negative models. A brother or sister can become an object of displaced aggression toward the parent. Such information further clarifies the patient's feelings toward a parent(s). Eliciting attitudes toward a brother or sister may also give you clues as to how the patient relates to the same and opposite sex.

The therapist should also explore the patient's feelings toward any immediate relatives, e.g., a grandparent who lives in or regularly visits the home. Similarly, the patient's reactions to a housekeeper or significant other person in the home rounds out the overview of the patient and his family adjustment. For example, realizing that a maiden aunt, who always lived in Cathy's home, and assumed the duties of a housekeeper, helped the therapist understand the pervasiveness and intensity of Cathy's sense of helplessness and rejection when she bitterly complained that even this aunt constantly "spied" on her. Like her parents, this aunt found fault with Cathy's dress, friends, school grades, ideas, and values. On the other hand, to cite another example, the type of support received from a close relationship with a relative gives hints for potentially healthier ego growth.

This was the case with Mark, a 17-year-old whose parents were divorced when Mark was 12. Unable to find acceptance and love from any of his relatives, parents, stepfather, or stepsiblings, Mark reacted in a self-destructive and passive-aggressive manner toward everyone. He withdrew from friends, became disinterested in the competitive sports in which he always excelled, adopted a pervasive indifference to life, and neglected studies which were always outstanding. One exception stood out clearly: a close relationship with a favorite uncle who made Mark feel secure and loved. With his uncle, Mark played tennis and sailed, visited other people, and conversed easily about himself. Until the therapist learned of this strong relationship and its positive effects on Mark, Mark was evaluated as an adolescent with a weak ego who had little inner strength and potential to cope with responsibility and growing independence. This preliminary evaluation was qualified significantly when Mark's relationship with his uncle was uncovered. Therapeutic strategy changed accordingly when the therapist realized Mark's rich potential for growth and untapped ego strength. Accordingly, the therapist engaged Mark more actively in therapy and confronted him sooner with his neurotic behavior. The highly supportive, indirect and cautious therapeutic approach that seemed initially indicated was no longer necessary.

To conclude this overview of important formative family influences, we want to share with the reader a question whose answer usually is most revealing of a patient's personality development: What person do you think has had the most influence on your life? Responses to this inquiry can be quite surprising, throwing into relief many subtle dynamic nuances. Especially important is learning the type or types of ego ideals or models the individual has incorporated. Often, the patient's reaction divulges more of the truer feelings and attitudes toward parents than the queries mentioned above. For example, asking the patient whom he admires most in the world, either a fictional character or world celebrity, can broaden the therapist's knowledge of the patient's hopes and expectations of himself.

Marital Relationship

With a married patient greater emphasis should be placed initially on collecting information concerning the marital rather than the parental relationship. Focus should always be on the patient's immediate home environment, and then on information regarding other personally close psychic environments. Therefore, with adolescents and adults still living with parents, emphasis should be placed on gathering data regarding the parent relationship. With the single patient living away from home, questions should concentrate on the immediate love relationship, if any, and then on the parents. As in seeking information about parents, questions about the marriage or love relationship represent an emotionally loaded psychic area.

Initial questions should gradually prepare the patient to express feelings toward the spouse and the marriage. This is best accomplished by an approach asking the patient to describe the wife or husband, and then shifting to a flashback or historical approach. What first attracted you to your wife or husband? What were your expectations of marriage? Your plans? Your goals? What were the topics of initial disagreement and how were they resolved? Understanding the marital background, especially major conflicts immediately before or early in the marriage, discloses much about the emotional climate of the marriage. To illustrate, in the case of 26-year-old Laura, her depression and acute insecurity become clarified upon learning of Laura's long-standing suppressed resentment toward her husband because of his last fling, a brief sexual affair while completing college before marriage. She never forgave him, and used this knowledge to reinforce a strong sense of worthlessness, and to nurse her repressed rage that fed into a masochistic character make-up.

Compatibility of the marriage partners is a crucial variable affecting marital happiness and success. What interests and activities do the marriage partners share? How is time spent together and apart? Around what issues are compromises made, and what emotions are aroused by the necessity for compromise? What kind of religious beliefs and personal value systems does each partner bring to the marriage? Reactions to these questions quickly help the therapist gain an appreciation of the compatibility and strength of a marriage.

For example, a marriage of two years was threatened by a patient's obsessive ruminations concerning her parents' marital problems. These ruminations caused Elaine, the patient, to question constantly her own marriage. Helping Elaine see that she and her husband shared many interests and activities, held similar values and goals, enabled Elaine to realize how very compatible they were. Thus, she was able to 1) gain strength from recognizing that her marriage was a good one; 2) grasp how she displaced neurotic reactions toward her parents onto her marriage; and 3) focus on the real nature of her present emotional distress, i.e., anger and guilt about her parents' chronically unhappy marriage, and a poor self-image.

Without genuine sexual gratification between husband and wife, a marriage will generate mutual frustration and resentment. Evaluating the patient's sex life will provide an index of marital fulfillment, and the patient's ability to intimately share himself with another human being. The therapist should inquire into the frequency of sexual satisfaction, i.e., attitudes toward orgasm and the frequency which it is achieved, and especially any changes in the partner's sexual reactions. Of great importance is the patient's initial sexual relationship with his wife which provides a base line to evaluate whether, and what kind of, changes have occurred with time. Finding out that Alan, the wealthy, self-made, 44-year-old corporate executive, had never achieved sexual fulfillment with his wife of 17 years, and that he has been prone to periods of impotency, helped the therapist understand a life-long inability to share himself with anyone in an intimate relationship. Moreover, that Alan's tremendous energy and total investment in his work represented the manner in which he sublimated the physical desires he could not gratify. Thus, light was shed on one of the reasons for Alan's overwhelming resentment toward his wife, and feelings of inadequacy that manifested themselves in Alan's social withdrawal and ineptitude.

While obtaining knowledge of the partner's sexual compatibility, it is timely to probe into the patient's early sexual experiences and attitudes if this information has not already been obtained from your questions about sexual development. In addition, the patient should be asked whether he has or is engaged in extramarital affairs. These questions allow the therapist to understand how the patient gratifies the universal need for love, as well as how he deals with issues of power and potency.

The capacity to accept others, possibly the most crucial variable in defining maturity, can be gauged by the marital relationship. Can the patient accept his partner's differences, and how does he accommodate for them. Does the patient allow independent thought and actions, or does he need to control and dominate? Can he compromise and accede to his wife's needs? Will he go to the ballet in which she is interested, or will he "first be caught dead" before he consents to his wife's interests? Such illustrations can be multiplied indefinitely and should be gathered by the therapist in order to evaluate the patient's ability to accept his mate. Incidentally, the authors' experience in working with marital couples has shown that the factor which most frequently generates serious marital discord is the inability of one partner to accept the other's need for individuality. Crushing a marital partner's need for self-assertion and demanding a submissive and unthinking attitude are the most destructive reactions one person can adopt toward another.

As part of evaluating a marriage, the patient's relations with his children should be explored. Questioning the patient about his expectations and problems with children may point to subtle signs of intrapsychic conflict. The patient as a parent will reveal hidden desires, frustrated wishes, and repressed resentments that can be gleaned from the type of relationship with his children.

Interests and Hobbies

The last category of information that we usually seek is an idea of what the patient does with his leisure time. What comprises his avocational and recreational pursuits? Cultural interests and hobbies divulge much about the patient's inner life, creativity, resourcefulness, and richness of personality functioning. The extent of emotional constriction can be measured

by the absence or presence of active interests other than activities relating to one's immediate work and family responsibilities. Also, are the satisfactions gained from the patient's hobbies
ego-enhancing or do they reenforce a particular neurotic trait?
Interests and hobbies may also suggest areas of frustrated goals
that could be used therapeutically to help the person grow in
more fulfilling ways. The discrepancy between a person's hobbies and his work may indicate an unacknowledged dissatisfaction with work. How the patient compensates for his failures
and unhappiness may also be reflected by the types of interests
he pursues.

Even if none of these dynamics could be suggested from
the patient's leisure-time activities, this information still provides the therapist with one invaluable piece of therapeutic
leverage: a clue to making contact with the patient. When all
else has failed in effecting positive rapport, discussing the
client's hobby will usually prove effective. Asking about and
showing interest in the patient's hobby can, surprisingly, overcome initial resistance and help the patient talk about himself.
Your interest in the patient's hobbies, which may mean more
to him than most everyday activities, lets him know that you
are truly interested in him. The wise therapist will keep this
knowledge, i.e., a particular hobby, in mind throughout the
course of therapy, referring to it as a means to open communication during periods of resistance and silence. By learning
more about the individual's job or hobby, a therapist can gain
a clearer perspective of his functioning and, more importantly,
develop additional avenues in reaching the patient. Making a
special effort, by extra study or research, to become knowledgeable about the person's work or hobby will reward the therapist
many times over with the improved understanding and rapport
thereby gained.

In summary, the foregoing case history outline touches on
the major developmental areas and life situations that will best
provide a thorough overview of an individual's dynamics and
present adjustment. This information will enable the therapist

to focus on the areas of major conflict and to understand the concerns of immediate importance to your patient. A precise and detailed case history will clarify your diagnostic evaluation and also offer a clue as to prognosis and the tempo at which therapy might proceed. Lastly, the therapist will find that the case history can point to significant leads to pursue as therapy unfolds.

DIAGNOSTIC PSYCHOLOGICAL TESTING

Arriving at a tentative diagnostic appraisal, or a definition of the problem and its dynamics, is a goal of the initial consultation phase. Psychological testing represents an important tool in refining the therapist's knowledge of the individual's intellectual and personality functioning. If the therapist is trained and experienced in administering and interpreting psychological tests, a session should be set aside for testing the client. Although there is some question regarding the advisability of the therapist assuming the role of the psychometrician, we have generally found this practice to be a valuable adjunct in evaluating the patient. Criticism of this practice revolves around the issue of threatening the client to an unwarranted degree by exposing him to tests, and thereby diluting your effectiveness as the sympathetic therapist-to-be. Rather, advise the critics, refer the patient to another clinician for psychometrics so that the therapeutic role is not impaired or diminished by the stresses placed on the patient from being tested. We have rarely felt that our role as therapists was diluted as a result of testing the patient during the evaluative process. On the other hand, administering tests, in addition to collecting the case history, often serves to demonstrate thoroughness to the patient.

The major issue is not the amount of stress or threat created for the patient, who is understandably anxious and uncomfortable during this initial consultation, but whether the therapist is competent and comfortable in administering tests as part of the diagnostic evaluation. If not, the therapist should then refer the patient to someone else for testing, but only if the therapist views the test results as being valuable assests. Not every therapist is sufficiently trained in diagnostic psychological tests to fully understand and effectively apply their results. Unfortunately, during the past decade there has been such an overemphasis on teaching clinical psychologists to become psychotherapists that their more traditional role as diagnosticians has been neglected. As a consequence, many psychologists, who are therapists, have not developed the diagnostic test skills that broaden their expertise in understanding patients.

Whatever your basic professional training as a therapist— psychology, psychiatry, or social work—psychological test results can furnish important information of the patient's level of intellectual and personality functioning that will supplement, clarify, and/or confirm your findings. Moreover, tests can provide important leads for therapy, and in situations where your impressions run counter to a test result, you may be on the verge of an important insight. A brief but meaningful test battery should include an intelligence test and various projective personality tests.* This type of battery will give you a measure of the patient's intellectual ability with specific reference to whether personality problems are impairing cognitive and learning processes. Too often, the therapist overlooks the significance of the patient's intellectual make-up, thereby never fully understanding the patient's educational or vocational adjustment. Projective personality tests can and should provide the following major facts of personality functioning: adequacy of ego development, defense mechanisms, major conflicts, degree of emotional control and responsiveness to others, level of

---

*A basic test battery should consist of a standardized intelligence test such as the Wechsler Adult Intelligence Scale for either Adults or Children, personality tests such as the Rorschach, House-Tree-Person Drawings, Thematic Apperception Test, Children's Apperception Test, Minnesota Multiphasic, perhaps an achievement test, and the Bender-Gestalt to add an understanding of academic achievement and perceptual-motor functioning.

anxiety, ego ideals, amount of striving, and degree of personality integration. Projective techniques will also offer clues to unconscious material that may not be suggested by interview techniques.

In preparing the person for the diagnostic tests it is best to be candid and informative. The patient should be told that these tests will provide additional information about his functioning that will enable you to obtain a more comprehensive evaluation than from the interview alone. Besides, the tests will offer knowledge that can enhance therapeutic process. Reference to test results, which should be shared discreetly, can be most effective when presenting your evaluation and recommendations at the end of the consultation process.

The informing interview or summary statement, which comprises your evaluation or diagnostic formulation and recommendations, concludes the initial consultation phase. Depending upon the complexity of the presenting problem, amount of material to be collected, and the responsiveness of the patient, this summarizing session will usually occur after the third or fourth interview. No fixed rule can be adopted regarding how much information should be imparted, but the therapist should strive to present an evaluation that has clarity, structure, and, above all, meaning to the patient. Patients want to know that the therapist has a grasp of the nature of the adjustment difficulty, and usually do not want a complex and overly detailed diagnostic presentation. Imparting a pedantic and intellectual description of the individual's problem is one way to lose him as a working ally.

THE INFORMING INTERVIEW

The most effective way to introduce the diagnostic evaluation is by indicating that your findings are based on many sources: case history, clinical impressions, results of the diagnostic tests, and information from previous professional reports, if any have been forwarded. The therapist's goal at this time is to inform the patient of the preliminary evaluation that will probably become more complete as the therapeutic encounter develops. We have found that a brief verbal summary of five or ten minutes touching on the person's major problems, which will be the focus of therapeutic help, is more than sufficient in conveying the diagnostic appraisal. How the patient reacts to this appraisal will usually reveal, to some degree, the validity of this assessment, and whether you have captured his interest and cooperation. When a meaningful and reasonably valid assessment is made, the patient will tend to react with verbal and nonverbal, (e.g., sighs, laughs, moans, blushes, shock-of-recognition) signs of agreement. Often, a sense of relief will be revealed because someone else finally knows what the patient has been suffering and keeping to himself.

Couching the evaluation in terms that can be accepted, i.e., nonthreatening, is of crucial importance. If the presentation evokes too much disagreement, indicative of resistance, or a finding that is not immediately pressing, you may lose the patient's faith in your skill and competence. The patient's puzzlement or disagreement over certain facts, however, may point to material that is too threatening and fraught with resistance; these topics should be noted for future discussion. Undue involvement by the therapist at this point with the disputed material could jeopardize the positive aspects of the relationship. If a patient is made to feel too threatened and uncomfortable by the therapist's remarks during this beginning stage, the patient has justifiable reasons for not beginning therapy. An attitude of care, sympathy, and desire to help must be transmitted while you are informing the person of your diagnostic evaluation. Caution must be taken to avoid transmitting any semblance of criticism, blame, or judgment. This can best be handled by directly telling the patient that in describing and summarizing his conflicts you are in no way being critical or judgmental, and that you are aware that what you say may be painful to him. An effective technique to make the appraisal acceptable is to use the same words as the patient when describing his symptoms. For example, we informed 31-year-old Joe that we saw his problem as consisting of an overwhelming sense of inferiority or a lack of self-confidence that prevents him from becoming independent and vocationally successful; his excessive worry about himself takes up all his energy so that he cannot concentrate and persist with any job or interest. We followed up these remarks with a phrase he initially used: "Joe, as you put it, you're 'on a negative road about myself.' " Elaborating on this, we told Joe that the findings explained the reasons for his "lack of accomplishment," and why he is prone to "flipping out" and a "hell with it all" attitude (phrases that Joe used repeatedly during the initial interview).

In addition to describing the patient's ineffective behavior (constellation of symptoms), the therapist must describe the extent to which the symptoms impair effective day-to-day behavior. To illustrate, by informing Joe that his present behavior will continue to create serious social problems, immobilize his energies, reinforce his passivity and dependence, and discourage him from working and developing job goals, we reenforced and confirmed the distress he had been experiencing. Patients want to know, and have a right to know, the effects of their neurotic behavior. As previously noted, this knowledge can induce a sense of relief in the patient because someone else has finally shared his fears and distress. Of equal importance is the effect of this diagnostic appraisal upon the therapist. It requires him to develop and maintain a rigorous disciplined approach that leads to a well thought-out initial evaluation. Furthermore, it prevents a sloppy, overly intuitive, "fly-by-the-seat-of-your-clinical-pants" approach (usually rationalized by having many years of clinical experience) that never achieves a focus to which the therapist and patient can address themselves. A focus and a structure have now been set which establishes the rationale and foundation for the therapeutic encounter.

We must note that this diagnostic appraisal should be presented not only to adult patients, but also to younger patients. Children and adolescents must be informed, but in language and degree of abstraction that will be modified and geared to their level of comprehension and emotional readiness. Moreover, the authors strongly recommend that the diagnostic formulation and recommendations be imparted to parents of the children and adolescents being treated. This does not mean that the therapist will betray the child's confidence. But too often therapists will ignore and neglect the parents' right to know because of an exaggerated notion of confidentiality. By properly structuring the diagnostic consultation phase, the therapist can let the child know that the parents will also be informed of the therapist's findings and recommendations after the evaluation is discussed with the child, i.e., the patient. This approach usually combats the child's anxieties about betraying confidences. The therapist should clearly emphasize that you will not discuss or disclose any of the content of your sessions with the child, but only will communicate your findings and recommendations to the parents. In fact, it is judicious to outline exactly with the child what you plan to impart to the parents, and to ask the child for his suggestions for the content of the informing parent interview. Sharing your findings with parents also gives you the opportunity of enlisting their help. Helping them understand the child's plight often clarifies their doubts, questions, and anxieties. And offering suggestions and practical advice with regard to their interaction with the child can aid the therapeutic effort.

RECOMMENDATIONS AND TREATMENT PLAN

After having outlined the nature of the patient's problems, the therapist is obligated to offer his recommendations that will, in essence, form the basis of the therapeutic contact. Elementary though it may seem, therapists are prone to forge ahead into therapy without explaining the goals of the therapeutic process. Consequently, it is not uncommon to find people receiving psychotherapy who are vague and unsure of exactly what therapy plans to accomplish. Patients have a right to know what the therapist plans to deliver. A person who sees his physician for hypertension, headaches, or hepatitis expects a cure, i.e., an alleviation of symptoms and improved physical health. A contract is made between the medical doctor and patient that implicitly or explicitly states that the individual will be cured or significantly helped to overcome a physical illness within a certain period of time. Similarly, the person who seeks therapy should be told in general what he can expect. Unless this is specified, the therapist will be failing the patient, as Strupp (1975) recently pointed out, and failing in our moral obligation as therapists. In fact, the statement of plan and goals (the therapeutic contract) can be likened to the truth-in-advertising concept. People come for therapy because they are suffering and need help (relief from their emotional dis-ease). The psychotherapist must explain the focus of his efforts and how he will provide this help. Everyone has a right to know what he is purchasing.

Therapeutic plans and recommendations need not be complicated and overly detailed, but highly specific and precise. Patients should be told that therapy will focus on their major adjustment difficulty and area of distress, e.g., phobic reactions, moodiness, feelings of inferiority, inability to assert oneself, violent temper outbursts, immobilizing depression, lack of friends, and so on. Therapists should explain which major problem area(s) will be dealt with and why. Also, as therapy evolves, goals may change as a consequence of progress, lack of progress, and greater information about the patient. Estimating a general timetable without implying a guarantee of success is also suggested. The patient can be told that, based on your past experiences and knowledge, change could occur within a specified time period (e.g., within six months), or that the nature of the problems indicate a long period of therapy. In any event, the patient should be informed that therapy is not a dead-end or interminable process, and that therapeutic progress will be reviewed and evaluated after a specified time period. This approach keeps in mind the outcome objectives and prevents therapy from becoming a fuzzy and intellectual exercise. If initial therapeutic goals change, a new contract can be renegotiated. Without this type of clarity, objectivity, and honesty, the therapist may involve the person in a time-consuming, endless, and costly venture to no genuine purpose. The therapist's first duty is always to the patient. In this instance, your duty is to make clear what the nature of the services are that are being sold and in clarifying what you cannot do. This open approach is especially needed today after decades of criticism that has viewed psychotherapy as a mystical, elite, and sometimes less than honest professional practice.

To close the circle, the authors firmly advocate that the therapist share with the referring practitioner or agency the diagnostic findings and recommendations for therapeutic intervention. This can be accomplished either informally by a telephone call or personal conversation, or formally by a letter. Not only is this a courtesy for their thoughtfulness in making the referral, but this information may be necessary in view of the referring individual's further contacts with the patient and/or his family. Besides, the therapist's appraisal may differ in many ways from the referral source who may, on further contact with the patient, influence the therapy in subtle ways.

For example, a general practitioner referred 17-year-old Dennis, who had run away from home twice in the past year and constantly cut most of his classes. The physician informed the therapist that he viewed the problem as just a sign of normal adolescent rebellion and was quick to note that the parents were overly understanding and affectionate. Also, how could such a thing happen to such "great parents"? Knowing that the physician treats this family, the therapist felt that it was important to clarify the physician's understanding of Dennis's problem. The diagnostic evaluation indicated that Dennis's passive-aggressive behavior reflected a deeply-rooted neurotic disturbance with emerging signs of a personality disorder generated by the emotional atmosphere of the family: unusual rigidity, a lack of communication, and a complete absence and avoidance of emotional expression by the parents. These parents literally bent over backwards to accept and understand Dennis's acting-out and antisocial behavior. They rarely displayed anger or any emotion other than a passive resignation. Dennis felt alienated from both parents and never gained a genuine feeling of security. These "good" parents never discussed things openly and were puzzled by Dennis's behavior. Running away from a home that bred instability represented a cry for help and attention, and an expression of intense hostility. Informing the referring physician that this was simply not a developmental adolescent phase, but serious neurotic behavior of long-standing and that psychotherapy would involve both Dennis and his parents, helped him understand the gravity of the problem. Therefore, the physician no longer harbored hopes, which he acknowledged, for an easy and quick therapeutic outcome, and he would be careful in not conveying such an impression to the parents whom he treats regularly. Last, he was most appreciative of the diagnostic information since it helped him appreciate the complexity of emotional disturbance, a reaction which illustrated the everpresent opportunity for educating others about emotionally troubled situations.

With the completion of the initial consultation phase, we are now ready to turn to the beginning stages of psychotherapy and its emphasis on defining the roles of the patient and therapist, the goals of therapy, and the crucial issue of establishing rapport.

Chapter 5

BEGINNING THERAPY

Strange as it may be, there are people who begin psychotherapy without understanding its goals and without knowing
what their roles as patients are. They have little idea of what
therapy is all about. When such ambiguity and confusion exists
in the person's mind, the fault can be attributed to the therapist,
who has not adequately prepared that patient for therapy. Developing and maintaining focus and structure, a recurrent emphasis of this book, is nowhere more important than in the
initial stages of therapy. The patient already knows from the
initial consultation the therapist's evaluation of his problems,
and what the general goal of the therapeutic effort will be. The
individual now needs to know what his and the therapist's role
is to be, and to understand something about the nature and
process of psychotherapy into which he is about to enter. This
is the time, at the threshold of therapy, when the therapist must
properly set the stage so that the therapeutic interaction that
follows is maximally effective.

Therefore, the patient should be informed immediately

that much of the first therapeutic session will be given over to describing how the patient and therapist will function and how therapy will proceed. So that the patient does not develop a mental set of expecting you, the therapist, to begin each session with a lengthy speech, we usually remark jokingly that this is probably the first and only time in a session where the therapist will talk so much.

GOALS OF PSYCHOTHERAPY

Describing the goals of psychotherapy is appropriate during the first therapy session. We inform the patient that psychotherapy sets three major goals for him, which we will pursue together in a working or therapeutic alliance.

First, for the patient to better understand himself; to gain self-knowledge; to see his strengths and weaknesses more clearly than ever before. Emphasis is placed on the rationale that by becoming better acquainted with oneself, the necessary foundation for change becomes established.

The second goal is to help the patient become the person he would more like to be. The therapist's role is not to tell the patient what he should become or what he should strive for, but to be the ally who helps the patient achieve these strivings. To illustrate, we note that the initial consultation has already indicated something of what needs to be accomplished and gained from therapy, e.g., to be less anxious, to be more effective with people, to be more self-confident, to become assertive, and so on, continuing with as many behavioral examples as appropriate to the particular patient. Stress is placed on the concept that therapy will help the patient become a happier person who will be better able to release and maximize strengths that heretofore have been held in check. This statement reflects the authors' strong belief, which was first emphasized by Carl Rogers (1964) that human beings possess within them a natural striving for health.

The third goal of psychotherapy is to arrive at some understanding of the obstacles or reasons that are contributing to the patient's maladjustment. An awareness of the dynamics or causative agents, knowledge which is synonymous with insight, may lead to quicker and more effective personality change and provide one with important guideposts for future behavior.

In clarification, the patient should be offered an illustration of an insight that can modify behavior. For example, the therapist may describe how a person's intense feelings of inferiority and anger toward others may stem from critical and unaccepting parents, and a desire to get even with them. During this discussion about understanding the reasons underlying behavior, the patient should also be made aware that insight, as all therapists unhappily know, is not always a sign of or necessary for change.

Psychotherapists should strive to explain concepts by offering anecdotes and examples in simple, everyday words. Speaking to the client in clear language and avoiding professional jargon will not only maximize the patient's understanding, but will force the therapist to think more clearly and precisely.

THE ROLE OF THE THERAPIST

After these psychotherapeutic aims have been set forth, the client needs to know something of the mechanics or operating procedures of psychotherapy. Defining the therapist's role is a logical beginning since first examining the therapist's function, rather than the client's, will least threaten the client during these early stages.

As therapists, we see our role as the ally and expert who will help the patient overcome his emotional suffering. The patient is informed that both he and the therapist are engaged in a search to find ways to solve his problems and that he can trust, confide in, and rely on the therapist. Whatever is talked about is confidential. Anything that the patient discusses and divulges will be accepted and not judged. Stress is placed on the nonjudgmental aspect of the therapist's role (a point that needs to be made over and over again as therapy unfolds).

As the patient talks of himself the therapist acts as a mirror reflecting back his words and showing him his typical mode of reacting to the world. The therapist explains that this is done to help him become aware of himself in an objective way so that he will gain a new dimension of self-awareness. The therapist prepares him for the fact that as therapy evolves, observations, interpretations, and explanations of his behavior will be made. Questions will be directed constantly toward helping him arrive at a new self-understanding. Neither interpretations nor questions will ever be made to judge, provoke, insult, or hurt him in any way. However, we let the patient know that he will not always accept or like what is revealed or said about his behavior and that he will not always accept or agree with our observations. Moreover, that resentment and anger may be understandably aroused by the therapeutic interpretations. The patient needs to be told and reassured that negative emotions and disagreements with the therapist are a natural ingredient of psychotherapy. These reactions will be dealt with and resolved as therapy continues.

While explaining the therapist's role as an interpreter of the person's behavior, this is the time to describe how difficult it can be to arrive at insight or understanding. Note is made that topics may be discussed over and over again in order to help the patient recognize typical modes of reaction, and that once this awareness (insight) occurs, therapy will help the patient apply this new understanding, i.e., work through the insight.

For example, after nearly nine months of weekly therapy sessions with 30-year-old phobic Sheila, which focused on her infantile and overly dependent relationship with her mother, Sheila announced that she has suddenly realized that she acts like a child with her mother. Also, that this fear of asserting herself and making decisions prevents her from being an inde-

pendent adult. As she continued talking about this new awareness, Sheila hesitantly explained that her phobia, which
prevents her from traveling and socializing, seems to have some
connection with this childish dependency. At this point, Sheila
realized how this dependency operates at all levels of her life as
a wife, daughter, sibling, and secretary. As she explored this
new knowledge and saw the harmful effects of this dependency,
Sheila gradually began to institute efforts to assert herself and
make her own decisions. This incident illustrates that it may
take a long period of therapy before the patient achieves insight
into an area that has been discussed repeatedly in therapy. And
when this insight occurs it must be explained and looked at
from many angles so that the patient can thoroughly assimilate
it.

Informing the patient that topics will be repeated and
examined from many viewpoints, and that achieving understanding (insight) can be an arduous and time-consuming task,
constitutes another approach in preparing the individual for
therapy. This explanation can alleviate the patient's expectations and anxieties that understanding and change should and/
or will occur immediately. For the therapist, this explanation
is a reminder that insight cannot be forced or hurried, and that
each patient has his own therapeutic rhythm or pace that the
therapist must respect.

THE PATIENT'S ROLE IN THERAPY

Although it may be obvious and simplistic, the patient
must be told that the context of therapy is made up of what he
chooses to verbalize. This fact serves as an introduction to
explaining the patient's role in psychotherapy. Unless the patient understands what is expected of him, his perception of
therapy may always remain fuzzy. It is our belief that therapy
will proceed more effectively if the individual has been prepared
and instructed in his role as a patient.

The most important point to convey is that you expect the patient to talk about his problems and concerns. The more freely the patient can express his feelings, ideas, and anxieties, the sooner will he become engaged in the psychotherapeutic process. Let the patient know that he is free to talk or not to talk, and that the more he talks and opens up the more effective therapy will be. Explain that he must develop a working alliance with you: the ability to look at himself objectively, to report his emotions, and to seek out ways to understand and overcome his problems. Although the therapist is hereby appealing for the individual's cooperation, the patient should also be informed that periods of resistance, or a refusal to become engaged, periodically emerge because of the threatening and upsetting nature of certain topics.

The major factor to stress repeatedly is that no matter what the patient may feel, whether it be threat, embarrassment, or resentment toward the therapist, he will best help himself by verbalizing these feelings. Without communicating openly, therapy can flounder and become ineffective. However, the authors recognize that every patient has his own rhythm and adequacy and ease of verbal facility. Therefore, patients will greatly differ in their degree of verbal expressiveness. Some individuals may be minimally verbal and even lapse into silences.

The author still vividly remember Elaine, a tense, thin, frail, and withdrawn high school senior whose therapy sessions for nearly a year were limited to verbalizations of no more than a phrase or single word during each session. Recognizing that Elaine's silences reflected a desperate need to assert herself, express intense resentment toward her parents, and to test the therapist's acceptance of her, we conducted the therapy sessions by alternating between periods of long silences and brief monologues which reflected back, described, and explained her behavior and remarks. Our patience and acceptance of Elaine appeared to have some positive influence as she eventually began eating again (Elaine was seriously malnourished and refused meals when she began therapy), returned to high school, gradually made a few friends, and tentatively began talking to her parents with whom she had refused to converse.

It is also wise, during the initial therapy sessions, to verbalize and sympathize with the patient's anxiety about self-expression. Accordingly, let patients know that it can be hard getting started and, if so, help the person by asking questions relevant to his cues and problems. You must be aware that this supportive and reassuring approach can backfire. The patient may count on your questions to resist and avoid genuine therapeutic involvement. If after several sessions, the patient still waits for your questions and does not spontaneously raise material, the therapist must then begin to cope with this as a form of resistance. On the other hand, the therapist must be able to differentiate between the fine line of resistance and a nonspontaneous, nonverbal, or inarticulate individual. Individuals who are submissive and nonverbal, yet eager for therapy, can usually be recognized by their cooperativeness in answering questions and addressing themselves willingly to whatever topic gets raised in the session. Resistant patients will maintain a superficial facade and evade responding to your inquiries. Nonverbal and passive patients, who are truly motivated for therapy, will become involved with you, and respond to encouragement and judicious questioning.

SETTING FEES

The practical details of the therapeutic contract represents the final or, perhaps for some, the initial state of defining the therapeutic relationship. The fee for therapy and billing procedures must be clearly set forth. It is our practice to inform patients that a monthly bill will be rendered, and that payment cannot be more than a month in arrears, and if so, the problem of finances must be discussed and resolved. We note that our experience shows that unpaid fees tend to create resentment in both the therapist and the patient. This situation will interfere with the therapeutic relationship. Every therapist faces, on occasion, the problem of unpaid bills, which must be resolved in some fashion if therapy is to continue unimpaired. This problem can be resolved by either terminating therapy or accepting the rationale for the delay in payment. The overriding principle is that the therapist must trust the patient and be sensitive to his ego needs. If you doubt the person's honesty and ability to pay, the therapeutic relationship will be harmed. It is best to confront immediately and openly the issue of unpaid fees by sympathizing with the person's financial problems and discussing other arrangements for therapy. The therapist should help the patient, in a supportive manner, to accept the fact that private therapy is beyond his finances and that there are community resources (e.g., clinics) where therapy can be obtained for a fee commensurate with his income. Most important, care should be taken to avoid expressing hostility toward the person and alienating him from further therapeutic help. When this situation arises, we recommend that the therapist assume responsibility for referring the individual to an appropriate resource.

Establishing Appointments

Making a regular weekly appointment time helps to maintain a certain rhythm and continuity in therapy and combats the problem of broken appointments. Patients need to know the therapist's policy regarding appointments. Our approach reflects the stress on accepting and understanding a patient's problems and being as flexible as possible. Our belief is that patients should be charged only for breaking an appointment (i.e., not showing up) if there has been no advance notice. Patients should not be charged if they have been prevented from coming by some unforeseen last-minute problem, e.g., a snowstorm, car breakdown, personal emergency, or if they have given sufficient advance notice. We tell patients that a day's notice is preferred for cancelling an appointment, but that several hours (4 hours) is acceptable. For the majority of patients, these limits will be sufficient. There will be patients, however, who will attempt to test the therapist around the issues of fees and appointments. Many, if not most, of the people therapists see have negative and/or ambivalent attitudes related to power and authority. The only real concrete power the patient has over the therapist lies in failing to pay fees or keep appointments. Some may experiment with this power by delaying payments and breaking appointments to ascertain how the therapist will respond. As a result, you may experience some diabolically subtle manipulations in this area. It is most important to be clear and firm, yet understanding and flexible. This is a difficult balancing act and your skill in dealing with these issues will increase with experience. Keep in mind that you will not be helping the patient by allowing yourself to be or feel manipulated without immediately dealing openly with this issue. The chief point to convey is that a therapist deals in time periods and that a contracted time must be honored or postponed sufficiently in advance so that the therapist can fill the hour and not be penalized, i.e., lose income. Similarly, patients need to know the exact length of a session. If they arrive late they will receive only their remaining time (or as the joke goes: you will start without them). On the other hand, if you begin late, the entire time will be given or made up at the next session.

The Therapist's Availability

Being available to the patient beyond regular therapy sessions is an issue that appears to arouse controversy among therapists. Some therapists seem to feel that encouraging or responding to the patient's telephone calls allows the therapist to be manipulated; therefore, these practitioners discourage calls and even avoid responding to them. Other therapists have no qualms about such calls and accept them as an inherent part of the therapeutic process, a view which reflects the authors' position. In fact, we believe that patients should be informed that they have a right to call the therapist whenever a problem or question arises that cannot be set aside until the next therapy session. Informing patients that you are here to help them and that they should feel free to call reflects our strong belief that as therapists we have an obligation to the patients that may, at times, go beyond the weekly therapy session(s). Crises do occur in every patient's life: a suicidal gesture, a phobic attack, a serious upset with someone important to the patient, a crucial decision to make, etc. It is our obligation and job as therapists to respond to a patient's call for help when a crisis arises, even though the crisis may only be a testing of the therapist's sincerity, i.e., will you really respond to me if I call you? Certainly, every therapist must be attuned to the possibility of a patient's need to manipulate, provoke, and to fulfill an insatiable need for attention, but these factors can be readily evaluated and resolved. Patients who abuse the right of calling can be helped to understand their inappropriate behavior and given firm limits. For example, patients who persist in calling after repeated explanations of your position can be told that you will not carry on a discussion when they call.

In the authors' nearly 30 years of combined experience in practicing psychotherapy, there have been very few patients who have abused the right of making telephone calls after the issue was discussed and limits set. We believe the true issue in setting limits on a patient's need to call reflects the degree to which the therapist is secure, open, and willing to give of himself. There are patients who will occasionally call and make apologies, believing that they are imposing. Our suggestion is to respond with approval and pleasure that they were able to discuss their concern with you. Every patient blossoms under approval and acceptance, and your reaction to a telephone call provides yet another opportunity to show that you care.

The Personality of the Therapist

Rarely do texts or articles on therapy discuss the behavior and personality attributes of the therapist. How the therapist behaves and relates to the patient is an issue that is crucial to therapeutic outcome. The authors believe that therapy fails more often than therapists would like to admit because of a failure in establishing effective rapport, rather than from a lack of theoretical knowledge. Perhaps some of the following remarks may appear naive, presumptuous, or too elementary to our colleagues. But they represent important, if not crucial, variables that every therapist should be ever aware of.

Most important is the manner in which the therapist shows his interest in the patient's problems. Therapy should be conducted so that the individual feels that you, the therapist, are interested in him and his difficulties. Therapists who are passive, affectless, overly controlled, and distant will have difficulty in conveying interest and concern to most anyone. Similarly, therapists who behave in a patronizing, know-all, and coldly efficient manner will not project a caring and accepting attitude. Therapists should be able to communicate a fairly outgoing, reasonably open, interested, and active manner to the patient. A therapeutic encounter is an exciting and challenging situation. It is not an occasion to bore the patient by an uninvolved, internalizing, constricted, and passive attitude. A sense of active involvement and dynamic interplay between the therapist and patient should characterize a therapy session. The therapist should feel free to make exclamations, curse, modulate his voice, joke, and engage in gestures and movements. An important qualifying factor, however, is to be careful that this active and involved approach does not overpower and squelch the person's spontaneity. Your reactions should allow the patient every opportunity to respond in his own rhythm and style. Moreover, the therapist must be able to maintain periods of "active" passivity, or as Reuben Fine termed in a recent lecture, "dynamic inactivity" in order to allow the patient to indulge his great need to talk and unburden himself.

The opportunity to talk to another human being who is interested in listening is probably one of the greatest benefits one can derive from psychotherapy. In our society one can readily talk to another, but whether one is truly listened to is questionable in this age of speed and superficiality which requires communications to be summarized in capsule form. The crucial differences between talking to a therapist and a sympathetic friend are that the therapist (1) is genuinely interested in listening in order to understand, (2) consciously refrains from imposing his values and advice, and (3) has the skills and knowledge to help the patient.

In recent years, the concept of self-disclosure has gained increasing acceptance as a psychotherapeutic technique. Disclosing personal information can be an effective technique to strengthen rapport or make a connection with a resistant patient. Self-disclosure, however, can easily be abused if it is not used judiciously. Telling the patient something about yourself should occur only as it arises naturally from, or is an organic part of, the topic being discussed.

For example, when the therapist described his own adolescent embarrassment and discomfort with facial acne to Ed, a teenage patient, whose severe bodily and facial acne caused him untold humiliation, Ed was able to feel our understanding and concern. This moment of self-disclosure lessened this patient's guarded and resistant manner and set the stage for the beginning of trust in the therapist. Here self-disclosure communicated the therapist's empathy. (The German "ein-fuhling" is the equivalent of empathy, literally translated as "feeling into another," best defines what the therapist must accomplish and convey.) Self-disclosure can be abused when therapists misguidedly speak about themselves as a way, usually without self-awareness, to impress the patient with their importance. All therapists are tempted with periodic thoughts of omnipotence and omniscience, and must struggle to maintain a sense of humility. When you find yourself talking about your accomplishments, interests, families, and personal matters, you are probably succumbing to the fatal flaw of hubris. Although every therapy session is, to some degree, inherently therapeutic to the therapist, it is not an occasion to indulge in neurotic and narcissistic gratification at the expense of the patient.

On the other hand, therapists are obligated to respond openly to the patient's inquiries about training, experience, and techniques. The consumer-patient has a right to know about your background. Such questions should be answered in a candid and positive way rather than handled in a defensive and resentful manner. The traditional attitude of "How dare the patient question me and my credentials?" has no place or validity in psychotherapy which is based on mutual respect and honesty.

A brief summary statement of your training, years of experience, type of patient problems usually treated, and techniques of treatment provide a sufficient answer to most inquiries. If your answers do not satisfy, and questioning persists, then you are dealing with a situation that is not indicative of just seeking information or feeling-out the therapist. You may be dealing with one or more of the following: excessive provocation, marked distrust, overintellectualization, obsessive-compulsive rumination, or a manipulative testing of the therapist. It is important that your answers to initial inquiries be brief and free from defensiveness. For example, when a teenaged patient asks if you have children, or if you have worked with drug abusers (or whatever), a straight-forward answer is all that is needed. However, behind those questions, in most instances, lie many needs besides obtaining information. Every therapist must be astute and sensitive enough to mentally note what other needs and dynamics these questions reflect, and to know whether they should be dealt with immediately, or as therapy unfolds. Is that adolescent patient also asking if you can understand his world, if you can be accepting, if you will be a parent to him, or if you will give him your exclusive attention? The challenge and thrill of therapy is to be constantly attuned to and aware of the subtle meanings and messages that lie behind most communications. Learn to listen with your "third ear."

Chapter 6

ONGOING TREATMENT

Every therapist must be fully knowledgeable and aware of the several basic concepts that pervade ongoing treatment and crucially affect therapeutic outcome. This chapter will be devoted to delineating the following key concepts: resistance, communication, continuity and focus, rapport, transference, and working through or changing behavior.

RESISTANCE

Resistance is most simply defined as those inhibitory forces within the patient that interfere with the ability to think, feel, act, and speak freely about the life issues being experienced and under examination. Resistance is based on fear arising from a variety of sources: fear of disapproval and rejection; fear of leaving old habits and the status quo; fear of change and something new; fear of having others discover the individual's inferiority in which the patient irrationally believes; fear of failure in attempting and maintaining change. This inevitable and perva-

112

sive aspect of therapy, more than any others, makes psychotherapy a difficult, complex, and protracted process, both for
the therapist as well as the patient.

Since resistance is an inherent characteristic of therapy
and connotes a negative reaction by the patient, we would
caution the therapist against viewing resistance only as a negative force. Resistance should also be seen as a positive trait; as
an attempt, however distorted, to survive and present oneself in
an acceptable way to others. Such a balanced view toward
resistance affirms the patient's potential for growth, and enables
the therapist to maintain the positive outlook necessary in practicing therapy. In essence, resistance reflects a fear of personal
annihilation, and a desire to survive unchanged. With this basic
understanding, consider the opposing forces available to deal
with resistance. First, there exists an equally powerful pull to
grow and experience. Next, there is the cognitive force which
seeks to learn and understand. Last, we have that part of the
neurotic system itself, i.e., the ambivalence, which reluctant-
ly desires change. These potentially healthy forces will provide some of the leverage the therapist needs to stimulate
change.

In dealing directly with resistance, the therapist must elicit
the patient's perceptions of the world in order to examine their
relative accuracy. Moreover, the therapist should understand:
how the patient acts on his perceptions; how they work for the
patient; and how they could work more beneficially. The patient's perceptual world must be viewed within the cultural
context that is neither "right" nor "true," but only the patient's
particular way of seeing things. Knowing, then, something of
how the individual sees reality, the therapist can proceed. One
of the basic rules in dealing with resistance is to do the unex-
pected. Do not play the patient's game by reenforcing the faulty
perceptual pattern. The patient has spent a lifetime in developing a social mask, a stereotyped system of perceiving and reacting to the world. Every patient plays roles and expects and
recruits others to play complementary roles. In the telling
words of Pearce (1974, p. 48):

Having adopted a protective mask . . . we forget that our lying (the mask) was an insulation against the accusations and irrationalities of our culture. We finally become or try very hard to become the mask itself.

The clinician's task is to show, help, and teach the patient that there are more beneficial and less restricting ways of perceiving and behaving. To illustrate this to the patient, the authors use the concepts of the "social persona" and the "inner persona." Most patients can relate readily to these ideas and will use them to distinguish between their public display and their private thoughts and feelings. By helping the patient recognize this duality, the therapist can draw out the person's genuine inclinations and inner motives, whose denial underlies the resistance. To aid in accepting the "real self," the spontaneous reactions the patient would give if the social mask were dropped, the therapist must create a climate of trust and acceptance. Without a feeling of trust, the patient will be too fearful to consider the possibilities of change.

Most techniques in dealing with resistance call for identifying and confronting the resistance. In a brilliant book replete with clinical wisdom, Greenson (1967) discusses the innumerable manifestations and psychoanalytic techniques in dealing with resistance. The other approaches consist primarily of "siding with the resistance," a technique pioneered by Nelson (1968). This fascinating and innovative technique advocates that the therapist agree or side with, as opposed to clarifying and contradicting the resistance. If the patient complains, for example, that everyone is against him or that therapy is not helpful, this strategy would agree with the reaction, rather than attempt to counter the distortion with logic or evidence. This technique seems to break through the stereotyped expectations and responses of the patient, and gradually forces behavior to change. In the authors' experience, siding with the resistance is a tricky but helpful tactic, if used carefully, and all its subtleties are fully comprehended. In siding with the patient's negative reaction, the therapist must have a plan and purpose. If the patient is denigrating himself, the therapist, in agreeing, must convey irony rather than condemnation. The entire strategem is ironic, and can often motivate quite resistant patients to begin defending themselves against their own negative comments; self-criticism turns to grudging acknowledgment of strengths and abilities. When the therapist agrees, patients may soon actually begin saying, "Well, I guess it's not really as bad as that . . . what I mean is . . . etc."

Another nonencountering approach to resistance is to do nothing. One of the hardest therapeutic skills is learning when to do nothing at all; to just listen, accept, and agree; to pass over the obvious problem without a reaction. Reusch (1961, p. 131) provides an excellent description of this technique:

> One of the most effective ways of dealing with pathology is to leave it alone. When the patient begins to mature, he has less need to rely on his pathology, and as time and energy are freed, he has time to cater to other but neglected personality features. As these functions begin to grow, the patient acquires new ways of gratification and the vicious circle is interrupted.

Time itself is another technique which does not directly confront the resistance. Often, it is the therapist's secret ally; or perhaps it just seems that way, because whatever the curative agent really is in treatment is often unknown to the therapist. As time passes, something usually happens; people tend to improve and the therapist is left to wonder and conjecture about what it was that worked in addition to the curative forces of insight, direct or indirect advice, suggestion, catharsis, and the caring therapeutic relationship.

The final technique in dealing with resistance is cultivating a therapeutic stance which demonstrates an unshakable affirmative attitude towards the patient's problems, abilities, and potentials. This attitude embodies a stubborn refusal by the practitioner to believe in the negative vision of the patient.

Whenever a patient tries to validate his negative vision, the therapist should acknowledge the reality (a school failure, a tragedy, a job loss, a divorce), but refuse to join the patient in his negative self-image. The clinician must be especially cautious to avoid reenforcing the patient's belief of being bad, deficient, and weak. Life is fraught with problems and requires constant struggle and effort to cope with adversity. This cannot and should not be denied or minimized. Human beings can, within realistic limits, succeed. What prevents most individuals from achieving fulfillment is believing in their own negative vision of things, their own resistance to change, risk, and growth. Often, many patients will know intellectually that their fears and inhibitions are exaggerated, but at the moment of action, are paralyzed by "believing" their distortions. Keep reminding patients that their negative vision is not shared by you. Imparting this belief alone can be quite therapeutic.

COMMUNICATION

Psychotherapy, like all human interaction, is based on communication. As a trained expert in communication, the therapist has attained some degree of mastery over its various forms. To help others, the therapist must discern the full flavor of the patient's experience by asking questions, listening, watching, and sensing. In the beginning phases of treatment, the clinician makes observations and forms a set of opinions about the individual patient. Sometimes these are accurate enough at the moment; sometimes not. Much depends on the skills of the patient in communicating and the skills of the therapist in observing and formulating. Our society is not an emotionally articulate one. Most people will have difficulty in allowing themselves to feel and react, and in describing what they feel and how they act. Helping such patients develop a system of describing and conceptualizing will often assist them in actually experiencing emotions. Frequently, one of the biggest blocks to feelings is a lack of knowing what to name them. Even those who seem able to feel with some spontaneity may be unable to articulate their emotions. This inability to express feelings usually leads to frustrations, anger, and isolation. Thus we can understand Chessick's (1969, p. 68) emphasis that psychotherapy is "an intensive training in the use of words to contain and convey the universe."

The task of the therapist is to define therapy as communication; then, to explain and illustrate this definition, act on it, and provide and promote an atmosphere that will maximize the development and exchange of communication. Since we define who we are by how others communicate to us and how we react and reply, it is important to establish early in treatment an active mode of communication. Many people have never verbalized their thoughts about life before therapy. Whatever fears and distortions previous experiences have generated tend to inhibit a free and open awareness of the world. Their capacity to perceive and use the potentially rich matrix of communication is nil. As one of our patients described it, they "sleep-walk" through the day.

To create an atmosphere that encourages communication, the therapist must set an example. The people we work with watch us. They see and sense how we deal with their remarks and conduct themselves accordingly. It is imperative, then, to demonstrate a warm, positive, patient, and accepting attitude towards what patients say and do. The fear of judgment and rejection, however disguised, is omnipresent. The fear which people have of being judged is often overlooked by the therapist, perhaps because it is so pervasive and common in therapy. Patients are continually on their guard, anticipating rejection or defending themselves against that probability. In a sense, this could be considered a thumbnail description of neurosis. The source of this anxiety is in the individual perception of self and others. As Reik (1956, p. 6) commented:

the child learns early in life to interpret the reactions of his parents or nurses as expressions of approval or disapproval, pleasure or annoyance. Being observed and later observing oneself will never lose its connection with this feeling of criticism.

Although the therapist initiates therapy with language, it is important to expand the concept of communication beyond merely speaking and writing. Communication covers the entire perceptual spectrum and includes every manner of giving and receiving information around and within us. Of the various senses, sight, hearing, and touch (including kinesthetic awareness) are probably the most important in therapy. This "nonverbal" level of communication has been the subject of considerable popularization in recent years as witness the emphasis on "body language," sensory awareness training, and the mushrooming interest in sports, martial arts, dance, and physical conditioning. Therapists should recognize that nonverbal modes of communication can be an important as verbal ones. When you consider how people relate to others, nonverbal communications vastly outnumber verbal ones. It is only a strange and slowly changing cultural bias that makes us think of most communication as consisting primarily of verbal facility.

To illustrate, one of the authors worked with Louise, a young woman whose difficulties, in part, reflected an identity crisis. She dressed and acted in a strikingly masculine manner although she expressed an admiration for and desire to be "more graceful," which she saw as "feminine." Sensing Louise's ambivalence about expressing "feminine" traits, the therapist encouraged her to attend a dance class, which she kept putting off, and suggested that when dancing, she attempt to let the "feminine" part of her dance. Being highly motivated as well as curious, Louise began dancing lessons and reported pleasure, surprise, and a "more relaxed feeling." Simultaneously, her symptoms of fatigue, depression, and excessive sleeping diminished rapidly; also, her dress and physical manner became noticeably less rigid and masculine. While much work remained in clarifying and working through the underlying dynamics, this device of encouraging nonverbal expression showed Louise other avenues of expression. More pertinently, it showed that change could be immediate, self-directed, and connected to her own thoughts about what could be helpful. If we listen closely and trust our intuition, the patient will often tell us what to do and where to start.

Other important nonverbal skills involve the use of imagery including fantasy, dreams, and intuition as valuable media for aiding the patient's expressiveness. The therapist should be aware of their usefulness in broadening his own proficiency as a facilitator of communication. In psychotherapy, the clinician works constantly at expanding the potentials within those he treats. It is consciousness expanding in the truest sense; developing connections and helping the patient to increase and be more aware of all types of communication. During treatment, the therapist explains and exposes the communication process; suggests and develops alternatives; and finally monitors and evaluates its development and outcome. Specifically, your major task is to assist people in expressing their experiences clearly and coherently. The therapist will, therefore, go over the same topics again and again, clarifying and refining the patient's experience of living. The curative effect of being able to articulate thoughts and feelings clearly remains the basis of successful psychotherapeutic treatment. And teaching our patients how to do so is one of the awesome mysteries of practice. "Finding the word" to express oneself can be and is a magical experience and often one that seems to lead directly to a greater sense of worth, mastery, and well-being. As Gendlin (1962, pp. 79–80) eloquently expresses:

> Often it is necessary . . . to invent some new way of speaking, in order to name some feeling. Sometimes not only a name, but a poetic image is needed. It is an important theoretical question *why* it makes so much difference to a person to conceptualize a feeling in

words that really convey it. However, in describing the experience of such conceptualizing, there is simply no question that it *does* make the feeling more intense, more clear, more real and more capable of being handled. The client feels as if he now knows where, in him, it is to be found. He feels as if he has grappled with it and now owns it, instead of being dogged by something partly unknown.

For the authors, there is no greater thrill than to watch our patients as they "grappled with it" and then with increasing skill, "find the words."

CONTINUITY AND FOCUS

Maintaining continuity and focus in therapy is closely connected to the concept of promoting and expanding communication. Again, these are simple ideas in concept, but maddeningly difficult skills for the clinician to master in practice. Contrary to the orderliness of textbook chapters, psychotherapy does not progress in an orderly coherent fashion by its own momentum. Similarly, the patient cannot be expected to bring to therapy a clear and well-focused body of information. Although beginning sessions can be filled with a recital of complaints and background, in a matter of weeks or months the patient may "run out of steam." "Everything" has been said, or at least said *once* within the patient's conventional framework of understanding and communication. At that point, it is usual for the first impasse to occur, i.e., "what is there to talk about now?" Here, the skill and training of the clinician come into play. It is imperative now to keep the communication going. Little or nothing can be gained by allowing sessions to flounder in frustration, storytelling, awkward silences, or the repetition of what has been said before. Our suggestion is to be active and encourage new verbalizations and modes of expression. For example, the therapist must question and elaborate the themes of the patient. Everyday experiences should be elicited and used to illustrate specific patterns and habits of the patient. Typical possibilities are questions such as the following: "How was the weekend?" "How do you spend a typical day?" "What has changed in your life?" "How are your relationships?" "How do you feel about what you just reported?" "What would you have done differently?" "If you could have said what you really felt, what might that have been?"

From the onset of psychotherapy, therapists usually have a general idea of the focus, the direction which therapy will take. Rather than impose that direction, the therapist should elicit material from the patient's thoughts and perceptions that will relate to that focus. To assist the patient and yourself in this regard, a clear and coherent focus and treatment plan are mandatory; also, a set of individual techniques that will pave the therapeutic path. Developing your own personal style is the hardest task for the novice and the continuing challenge for the experienced clinician. The authors' advice is to model yourself after other admired therapists. Read as much as you can about psychotherapeutic technique both within and outside of your chosen therapeutic orientation. No school of therapy has yet cornered the market on effectiveness. But within each there are demonstratively effective practitioners and a plethora of effective techniques. Discover and try them if they harmonize and support your evolving style. In the words of Lazarus (1971, pp. 32–33)

> The best therapy is that which works for the individual . . . The most essential ingredients for an effective psychotherapist are flexibility and versatility . . . the ability to play many roles and use many techniques in order to fit the therapy to the needs and idiosyncracies of each patient.

In tandem with striving to learn, develop, and experiment with the techniques of others, comes our second dictum: invent. Do not be afraid to follow a whim or intuition. That is how techniques are born and how the experienced professional decides when to use a particular one at a given time. During the course of listening and speaking with patients, you will have thoughts and impulses come suddenly into awareness. Usually these will be spontaneous and personal associations to what is being discussed. These can be characterized as intuition which can be a rich source of innovative response. Reik (1956) described a similar process as "listening with the third ear." This technique is based on trusting the efficacy of your own unconscious and reacting with hunches below the threshold of immediate awareness. Learn to trust this intuitive technique in everyday practice which is illustrated and described throughout Reik's classic book.

A cardinal rule in maintaining continuity and focus is that therapeutic exchange must always focus on the needs of the individual patient. As Carl Jung (1964, p. 66) advised:

> The knowledge of human nature that I have accumulated in the course of sixty years of practical experience has taught me to consider each case as a new one in which, first of all, I have had to seek the individual approach.

Once you have identified the individual issues, stay on them. It is deceptively easy to stray from the focus and the treatment plan. For the beginning practitioner, it can be difficult to switch gears from one session to the next; when one patient walks out the door and another walks in. When the focus unravels, when the direction strays, bring it back. There are some basic, simple techniques that can be overlooked easily. For example: "Well, I see the issue as . . .", or "I don't understand, how does this relate to your difficulty . . . what we were discussing was the issue of. . . ." Another helpful technique is to buy an appointment book that has space for short notes for each session. Furthermore, remember the resistance that always operates. The practical, tough reality is that the patient may not want to talk about the issues that trouble him beyond a superficial level. He will avoid them, deny them, talk around them, and generally find some tangent to take. Bring the patient back gently, respectfully, subtly, but consistently to the focus from which he has strayed.

Another rule in maintaining continuity is repetition. The nature of psychotherapy is that problems are simple and solutions difficult to structure and accept. You will by necessity cover the same ground, on different levels, over and over again. Never be reluctant to repeat. The measure of your evolving clinical skill will be how well you can maintain your focus *and* the patient's concentration in the face of constant repetition. Make this clear to your patients. Do not let it go unarticulated or be "understood." It is an unwritten rule of social conduct that one must never be repetitious and boring, never talk about the "same old things." Psychotherapy is not social intercourse, and it should establish an atmosphere in which patients understand the necessity for repetition and review of experiences, thoughts, and emotions.

Finally, the other side of the coin of continuity: Focus and refocus, or *know where you are going.* Remember, if you do not know, nobody does. Or more accurately, the patient knows but is not sure he wants to go through what he has to in order to get there. It is the therapist's responsibility to provide the structure of treatment. This is why we are trained and what we are paid to do. The therapist is not merely a sympathetic listener, a surrogate friend, or parent; he is a healer, a professional, an expert, someone who can help.

The best method for maintaining focus is clarification and periodic review. The psychotherapeutic relationship is an ongoing process, and patients, therapists, and the environment changes. Nothing remains static. The most difficult and resistant patients change, even if only to become worse. In treating a patient for any length of time, the constant pull is to unfocus and get sloppy; an understandable human response to repetition and frustration. Attention wanders, fatigue sets in. Think of the incredible amount of verbal and nonverbal material produced by both participants over a period of time. To make sense out of all this material, the clinician needs a system, a method of focusing and clarifying. We subscribe to the method that constantly seeks to organize facts into a pattern. In the words of Angyal (1965, p. 216):

> The therapist who develops the habit of constantly relating single items to general patterns will reap the benefit of improved memory; organized material is remembered better than unrelated detail.

In addition to this technique of searching for behavior patterns, there must be periodic review to maintain focus. The therapist should review periodically what has been discovered, learned, and changed during therapy. From this review, the participants can determine whether any alteration in focus or direction is indicated. While reviewing therapeutic status, progress, and goals, it must be remembered that the patient is an active participant in the review process and not just the recipient of information. It is the patient who is, in reality, the final judge of whether to continue, change, or terminate therapy. After many years of using this technique again and again, we are still surprised how effective it is in clearing the psychic cobwebs, reinvigorating, and reestablishing the creative continuity of the therapeutic process. The smallest amount of energy spent on focus will repay both therapist and patient many times over in maximizing therapeutic efficacy.

THE THERAPEUTIC RELATIONSHIP AND MAINTAINING RAPPORT

> The therapist listens and tries to understand. Then (by habit, but at first deliberately) he attempts to feel for himself sharply the "feel" of what the client is communicating . . . At appropriate times, when the client has finished for the moment, the therapist will respond *from out of* this "feel" that has been forming while the client spoke (Gendlin, 1962, p. 83).

Psychotherapy is an art of nuance and a craft of indirection. Teaching, learning, and describing therapy all too often omits what we know or want to find out. Usually we end up speaking in metaphor, poetic allusion, anecdote, stratagem, and intuition. Accurately describing the process usually seems beyond the limits of spoken and written language, especially of what almost all writers on psychotherapy have characterized as the essence of our work: the relationship and rapport of the therapist with the patient. To speak meaningfully on the therapist–patient relationship requires that we consider the mystery of physical, mental, and spiritual existence. All human beings are essentially unknowable, they are an infinitely complex system of attributes, reactions, motives, contradictions, and paradoxes. Despite our complexity, we are all in some concrete way whole and complete. The miracle of life, beyond the immense body of scientific knowledge about its function, remains awesome, frightening, yet somehow exhilarating. How then, do we propose to comprehend and interpose ourselves as "psychotherapists," in a helping and healing way, into the lives of those who seek us out? This is an attitude that places the whole before the parts, the total experience of living before the artifacts of life, and that looks for the underlying health before the details of pathology. This "attitude" also shows profound respect for the individual vision and the right of the patient to be himself. On this foundation, our work is built. Realistically, we will violate this precept repeatedly in our personal lives as well as in our professional endeavors. This is unavoidable, since we are less than perfect, but as Coleridge wrote: "Goals are like stars, they can never be reached, but we set our course by them."

Practicing therapy involves not only a knowledge of specific skills, but an ability to apply them creatively. The following illustration will clarify this emphasis: In preparing this text, we noticed that writing is divided into two different tasks: first, the mechanics of research, copying, collecting, typing, proofreading, indexing; second, the creative art of the actual writing. Similarly, psychotherapy can be performed either as the background detail work or as the creative act. The difference rests in your attitude and goals. The mechanics or details comprise your training, discipline, skill, and technique. The creative act is the integration of the details into your personal vision and committment to help and to heal. To stimulate and foster this developing creativity, prepare for your sessions. Not the usual preparation of reviewing notes and supervisory advice. Rather, think about what you are doing with each patient; why are you doing it; what you hope to accomplish. Consider the effect practicing therapy has on you, especially the responsibility of healing others. These can be frightening and humbling thoughts. Face them by recalling what you have accomplished, and give yourself some positive feedback and encouragement. You too are "in therapy" many more hours a week than any single patient. As you consider an individual patient, review the progress of your relationship. Evaluate what works and does not work within the evolving rapport. Weed out difficulties; "feel" them. Are you comfortable with a given person? If not, why: What are the problems in relating? Remind yourself of your limitations. Refresh your grasp of the therapeutic contract and the vectors of responsibility. Meditate on the individual differences which exist in you and each person you help. Remember Frankl's (1963, p. 123) advice:

> No man and no destiny can be compared with any other man or any other destiny. No situation repeats itself and each situation calls for a different response.

Looking at the practice of therapy in this manner can provide you with a more profound, flexible, and spontaneous grasp of your work. Just one warning. Do not make a ritual of preparing for each session as the process will quickly lose its spontaneity and effectiveness.

In the therapeutic setting, never forget that you are a human being relating to humans who are patients. Do not expect the same person each time, even with those who share similar symptoms and patterns. Function with the knowledge that the largest part of maintaining rapport is in dealing with each individual person, not as a "case" or a constellation of symptoms. Above all, avoid getting hooked into pathological perception that is self-generating and self-reenforcing. If you look for disease, you will find it, even in your friends and yourself. Look instead for the patient's strengths and health. By no means ignore the difficulties, but do not dwell on them exclusively. An ancient Indian aphorism is here relevant: "When a pickpocket looks at a saint, all he sees are his pockets." Look at the whole person. We are not merely psychological pickpockets.

Another technique in relating effectively is that of "self-disclosure." Surprisingly, controversy still surrounds its use. Objections for its use stem from traditional psychoanalytic notions of the analyst as the "mirror of transference," and from the reluctance of many therapists to have their patients possess personal knowledge of them. We submit that this latter objection concerns itself more with the limitations of the therapist than with concerns about the ramifications of self-disclosure to the patient. Self-disclosure can be a powerful tool, nevertheless, and should be used with discretion. As a rule of thumb, you may respond to a patient's question about yourself with the same, simple, and straightforward replies you would give in normal social situations. Lazarus (1971) provides and excellent discussion and illustrations of dealing with such inquiries. Keep in mind, of course, how the content and context of the questions relate to the patient's attitudes and feelings about you and therapy. Therefore, the therapist should follow up his responses by questioning the patient about his reason for wanting to know personal information. In most cases, however, it is best to accept the queries as a sign of normal curiosity, and not treat them as the patient's aberrant behavior.

In addition to answering personal questions, self-disclosure can be used effectively in other contexts. When a patient is describing an experience that triggers a similar memory in the therapist, it can often be helpful to briefly relate your own experience. Sharing a similar incident is done primarily to make a point and show the patient the commonality of human experience. For example, the therapist may wish to indicate that the patient's anxiety was exaggerated, that these things happen to many people, or to show some alternative ways of dealing with the problem. The caveat is that self-disclosure must not, in any fashion, deprecate the patient's sense of worth. It should not be used to show how superior the therapist's insight and behavior are. Self-disclosure must be oriented to the patient's benefit, not the therapist's ego gratification.

To illustrate, one of the authors recently treated Susan, who was describing her intense discomfort at the funeral of a relative. She felt that many relatives and friends were displaying a "melodramatic" show of grief which contrasted sharply with their previous uncaring attitude toward the deceased. The patient's anxiety resulted from other factors besides the "phony display": her impulse to expose the hypocrisy; her anger at the deceased when he was alive; and her traumatic reaction to the death which she observed. In response to Susan's agitated remarks, the therapist sympathized with her feelings by describing our own ambivalence toward funerals, especially our anger toward people showing grief that was hypocritical and merely for public display. This disclosure helped to relieve Susan's guilt and anxiety about her own feelings as she stated, "I guess I'm not the only one who feels like that." Establishing this empathic bond enabled us then to more easily explore the dynamics behind her guilt and anger.

The issues of love and caring constitute another significant aspect of the therapist–patient relationship. Psychotherapy involves an intense emotion between patient and therapist; however, the intensity and quality of emotion will differ markedly between the two participants. This imbalance is unavoidable, and must be handled with subtlety and discretion. Probably all patients during treatment experience mixed feelings of affection and "love" for their therapists. These feelings can extend themselves to the erotic level. Our view is that while we must truly care about all of our patients, we act unethically and irresponsibly if a sexual relationship with a patient occurs. Occasionally, a strong affection for a patient may develop that is continued beyond termination of treatment. However, rarely does a former patient become a friend.

The principle of caring is the crucial point in relating effectively to patients. The successful clinician develops the facility of finding a characteristic of the patient to admire and appreciate, and the ability to communicate a sense of acceptance. Unless this can occur, psychotherapy will become an academic exercise, without true involvement, and devoid of any pleasure for the therapist. This can be a true test of the therapist's maturity as it challenges the therapist to care genuinely for people who will continually test and attempt to destroy your caring. Every therapist must learn to separate the person from his actions, to care even though you do not care for the patient's behavior towards you and others. Through caring, the therapist can provide, perhaps for the first time for a patient, a positive adult relationship which will validate the healthy strivings of the individual. Angyal's (1965, p. 18) words beautifully convey this emphasis:

> The true human problem is this: in a sense that matters to us above everything else, we are nothing in ourselves. All we have is a profound urge to exist, and the dreadful experience of non-existence . . . A man in the most crucial way is a symbol, a message that comes to life only by being understood, acknowledged by someone.

In the words of a canny old therapist of our acquaintance, caring involves the ability to both "hold hands and kick ass." Therefore, we see caring as far more than a benign acceptance and appreciation of everyone's humanity. True caring and sophisticated skills require more than unconditional acceptance.

Negative and destructive behavior should not be accepted unconditionally. Indeed, it must be questioned and confronted by the therapist whenever it occurs.

Acceptance and caring can be demonstrated in many ways. The literal "holding of hands" in moments of deep anguish or sorrow can communicate more than a thousand words of consolation or interpretation. With sensitivity and discretion, patients may even be physically embaraced on occasion. The authors have a custom of sending greeting cards on special occasions such as births, graduation, or marriage. Many other gestures of relatedness are appropriate including the occasional taking or offering of refreshment when it occurs naturally in the setting, sharing a joke, or expressing sympathetic feelings. For how and when to do this, listen to your inner sense of appropriateness and be sparing. Never use these as "techniques," but rather as a sincere and personal expression of yourself.

A more difficult question is when to "kick ass" or confront the patient with his destructive reactions. Again, there is no specific technique here, only the skilled and developed experience of the practitioner. Most obviously, it is the therapists's responsibility to retard and, if possible, prevent the patient from harming himself and others. The key concepts to follow are flexibility and versatility. When the standard therapeutic work of uncovering, interpreting, and building alternatives appear to make little headway in overcoming some serious behavioral maladaptation, often a sharp, direct but concerned and non-rejecting confrontation may break the deadlock. Many of our patients have said, following such incidents, "You know, the time you yelled at me was probably the most important session I ever had." The key to success with this approach depends upon 1) the quality of the rapport and 2) selecting the appropriate time. Thus, the therapist must establish the proper conditions in order to make such confrontation effective. Nonetheless, it is a very powerful tool and should not be avoided because it is delicate to use. Learn to trust your feelings and begin to test them. Intuition is a skill that can be trained like any other skill.

TRANSFERENCE

In traditional psychoanalytic therapy, transference describes the process whereby the patient inappropriately and unconsciously displaces onto the therapist reactions based on past experiences. Thus the patient reacts to the therapist in terms of his past history, and thereby distorts and misunderstands the present therapeutic interaction. For example, the patient will see the therapist as a disapproving parent and react in terms of that distortion.

Our belief is that transference is a much broader principle, a universal phenomenon that occurs not only in therapy but operates throughout life. Transference should be understood to include the present as well as the past, the conscious as well as the unconscious. In a sense, transference reactions indicate the manner in which the individual patient relates to others. From our earliest beginnings in life, we look to someone who can make us feel sage, strong, and protected, to help us overcome our feelings of impotence and inadequacy. And in therapy, the individual tends to relate to the therapist with similar expectations. However, our broader emphasis is that every patient also reacts to the therapist in terms of the here and now, or in Angyal's (1965) words, the "real relationship" with the therapist. Not only the historical past but the immediate present influences the patient's reactions. Consequently, transference is neither just a negative or a positive process. It can fluctuate quickly or gradually from negative to positive depending on the meaning of a situation for the patient, the meaning that is derived from the patient's past, and/or the meaning based on the realistic perception of the therapist in the here and now. The transference reaction should, therefore, not be seen as a sign of a disturbed frame of mind, but rather as an expression of a natural, organic process which reflects how the patient perceives and reacts to others and the world at large.

The therapist must be constantly aware that he will be perceived inevitably in some faulty, idiosyncratic, or distorted manner. Usually, the distortion will be a positive one, an idealization. A positive reaction will be helpful in developing a positive rapport that allows the therapist to exert a constructive influence. Specifically with transference reactions, the therapist must point out the kind of distortions and aid the patient in correcting them. Correcting the faulty perceptions of the patient should always be directed toward helping the patient deal more realistically with everyday life situations, especially helping the patient understand how his unrealistic positive or negative perceptions influence his interaction with others. When the transference remains consistently negative or when the patient relates only negatively, the outlook for favorable therapeutic progress is usually poor.

Countertransference is the clinician's transference reactions to the patient. Like transference, it is an inevitable and universal phenomenon which follows the same characteristics as transference. Every patient will elicit distorted responses from the therapist. Countertransference requires constant vigilance and awareness. In the wise words of Menninger (1973, p. 93):

> One must be constantly alert to the existence of countertransference, but not intimidated by it, recognizing both its pitfalls and its uses. . . . Think about it from time to time; reflect on it . . . For countertransference is dangerous only when it is forgotten about.

To best implement this advice, the beginning therapist should seek competent supervision to discover the faulty perceptions that are by nature difficult to uncover and clarify. Like all therapeutic skills, understanding the countertransference and dealing with it takes time, experience, and discipline.

The entire issue of countertransference eloquently points up the balanced or relational nature of psychotherapy. Therapists are not surgical instruments, electronic devices, facile techniques, or encyclopedic cookbooks. However skilled, therapists are human with a vulnerability that is both a strength and a potential weakness. The relationship and rapport with patients cannot be taken for granted. It must be carefully built and assiduously tended. Like a garden, it will bear fruit in direct proportion to the skill and caring that is brought to the task.

Developing Understanding and Insight

As noted earlier, our society is not an emotionally articulate one, despite the increasing pseudo-sophistication of the general public in psychological matters. An essential task of psychotherapeutic treatment is to identify the difficulty most people have in expressing emotions and demonstrate its importance to each patient. Therapists must help individuals to express feelings which have been internalized, denied, or rationalized. This process is analogous to learning any communication skill, and requires "building an emotional vocabulary." Although special emphasis should be placed on this task in the beginning stages of treatment, helping patients express emotions is an ongoing process. How this goal is accomplished varies with individual practitioners. Several basic techniques and key concepts are useful: repetition, clarification, exploration, and elaboration. In therapy, as in life, we go over the same ground again and again. Developing skill and pleasure at this task involves finding different ways to talk about the same material. Take advantage of the rich imaginative and intuitive powers of the patient and yourself. Encourage the use of different words, the use of analogies and examples, associations, and just plain story telling and imagination. Never be afraid to repeat the same issue. There can never be enough repetition; if it is verbalized differently, it demonstrates the underlying patterns of behavior.

Clarification, exploration, and elaboration are really part of the same process. When you elaborate, use different words to express the original idea. When you explore a thought, try to give examples. It is all part of the attempt to get as much therapeutic mileage out of the material elicited in therapy. Often, the real difficulty for the patient is not the lack of therapeutic material, but not knowing how to make use of this information in real life. In a comprehensive book on therapeutic communication, Reusch (1961) terms these and similar techniques "therapeutic dialectics," which include: pinpointing, documentation, translation, comparison, contradiction, confrontation, argumentation, analysis, and synthesis.

All of these techniques can be subsumed under the principle of interpretation which is the process aimed at helping the patient to acquire insight or an understanding of his problems. Insight aims at introducing new elements into the patient's psychic system, altering the status quo, and producing a new synthesis of self-perception. With interpretation, the most difficult issues revolve around timing and judgment. During ongoing treatment, every patient will be filled with ideas, associations, and questions raised by the therapeutic material and therapeutic interaction. For both the novice and the experienced therapist, the easiest trap is making too many interpretations too quickly. The novice will often respond like the nervous cowboy firing at anything that makes a false move. This will frequently result in premature, poorly planned, and fragmented interpretations that will impede progress and may impair the therapeutic relationship. Usually, such interpretations are harmless and most patients will ignore and deny them. Occasionally, however, a profound but untimely interpretation can overwhelm a fragile patient's defenses and precipitate enough anxiety to cause termination of therapy, and, in rare cases, personality decompensation. In any case, the therapist is expending much effort with little effect, and the patient is being confused, causing frustration for both participants. Here, the clinician must actively control his zealousness and stifle the impulse to "get someplace" right away.

The therapist should always be aware of the power behind the patient's inability to see and grasp the core issues of his or her difficulties. If information alone were sufficient, psychotherapists would soon be out of business. Remember that the patient's distortions and symptoms fulfill a palpable psychic need. No neurotic attitude or behavior can be removed without being replaced by something that performs equivalent psychological "work." An interpretation that threatens to leave behind a structural vacuum *must* be avoided. If such a vacuum occurs, the whole personality structure may be threatened with collapse.

For example, in the beginning stages of therapy, a patient, Joan, described her mother as self-centered, uncaring, manipulative, and dishonest. Joan poured out her intense rage, contempt, and distrust of her mother, citing numerous anecdotes to show that everyone felt the same anger toward her mother. As therapy progressed, Joan revealed traits which were strikingly similar to the mother's behavior. We refrained from making this interpretation since the rapport was not sufficiently established to cope with such a threatening observation. Instead, therapy initially proceeded to be supportive and to build up a more positive self-image as a buffer for future confrontations.

The most effective interpretation will combine the past, present, and therapeutic context into a meaningful whole. Such an interpretation places the interpretative information within a framework of known issues and adds new knowledge.

To illustrate, after several months of therapy, 30-year-old Sid remained noticeably passive, constricted, and fearful in a manner that prevented any self-assertion and expression of feelings. An apologetic mood pervaded Sid's remarks which he verbalized with much reluctance and great effort. He rarely looked at the therapist while speaking and constantly grimaced as if in pain. His entire demeanor and mood reflected intense discomfort and a need to be constantly on guard. As we talked of his teenage years, Sid began to complain about his parents' ineffectual, weak, and helpless attitude toward life. He feared becoming like them and resented their oppressive influence. Sid's overwhelming resentment erupted during his college freshman year when his father became increasingly critical and disapproving. With much guilt, Sid reported that the argument led to a brief exchange of blows which terrified him. Following that fight, Sid became more passive, submissive, and fearful; intensification of personality constriction puzzled him. The therapist gradually realized that Sid's continued discomfort with therapy, the chronic lack of self-assertion, and severe difficulties in expressing emotions reflected not only a fear of disapproval and reprisal, but, more important, indicated a terror that his emotions would overwhelm and destroy him. Sid was terrified that his murderous rage would become uncontrolled and destroy him if he allowed himself to express genuine emotion. This interpretation connected 1) the past or hostility toward disapproving and ineffectual parents, 2) the present extreme submissiveness and fearfulness which protected against the murderous rage, and 3) the therapeutic context or the inability to relax and to relate genuinely because of the imagined fear of reprisal and disapproval. In this interpretation and further discussion, the therapist worked at improving Sid's reality perceptions by showing him that expressing emotions would not lead to a loss of control, murder, and reprisal; while clarifying the distortions, the therapist constantly used his relationship to the therapist as a model.

Another technique is recommended to lay the groundwork for interpretations. Rather than explaining the patient's behavior to him, have the patient explain his behavior to you. The more behavior is expressed in the patient's words instead of the therapist's, the better the chances for grasping and integrating that insight. This takes more time and focus, and requires patience. Finally, when an interpretation is made, the therapist must document it with behavioral examples. The best documentation will not be found in the therapist's conjectures, but in the patient's own words and reports. The entire process of developing insight and self-understanding is focused on helping patients gain a sense of their own history and identity, and a feeling for their roots. Being aware of this knowledge and its influences promotes an appreciation of the here and now. For most people, the past is a jumble of isolated memories and impressions, coupled with a vague awareness that something is wrong and a sense of confusion as to who they are and how they got to their current predicament. To have a clear sense of your history promotes the experience of belonging and centeredness. It is finding your inner "roots."

Every therapist must be aware that insight alone seldom produces lasting change. Insight and understanding can only set the stage for change. Insight tends to imitate and support changing behavior, but it is not change in itself. The novice must especially take care not to confuse the two.

CHANGING BEHAVIOR/WORKING THROUGH

The goal of psychotherapy is the changing of behavior. What these changes will or should be varies with each patient and therapist. But in almost every case change in behavior must occur for otherwise treatment will have failed. In most instances, the necessary changes in behavior will be obvious to both participants. However, there may be substantial difficulties between the perception and realization of change in many cases. To help make the process of behavior change simpler and clearer, the following thoughts and recommendations are offered.

The first idea revolves around understanding what can and will be changed in therapy. Almost without exception, the distressed individuals who seek therapy prefer to change their feelings rather than their actions. There is a persistent illusion among laymen (and a few professionals) that emotions can be manipulated directly, changed, and modified; that what psychology does is to take away "bad" feelings and replace them with "good" ones. Nothing could be further from the reality we have experienced as therapists. How and what we feel is beyond our control. When we are feeling it, we have no choice but to feel it. Most patients, however, will deal with emotions as if they were as tangible as behavior. They want to have "good or desirable feelings," and not have "bad or undesirable ones." This notion that some parts of us are good and others bad is at the root of all neurotic behavior. The attempt to deny or disown aspects of our inner experience because the emotions and ideas are unacceptable to ourselves or to others results in emotional disorder. The therapist should emphasize throughout treatment that patients must learn to accept their emotions, however strange or distasteful they may seem. Patients need to understand that they have choices to initiate action and change behavior, but that emotions cannot be changed. We can choose to act in ways that elicit certain feelings, but we cannot choose the emotions we have.

Working through, then, begins with helping the patient accept his thoughts and feelings, and proceeds to identify the behavior which might be altered. The therapist accomplishes this by setting an example of understanding and acceptance, and by providing a therapeutic context within which to examine new and old ideas and actions. This context or therapeutic approach can and does vary infinitely among therapists. In our experience, what is more important than the type of approach or context is that it be coherent and consistent. The therapeutic context must provide a stable ground from which a patient may examine and assess his life. Since the neophyte therapist has no carefully constructed and well-developed therapeutic context, this situation becomes the single most difficult dilemma for the beginning practitioner. This dilemma is akin to being a carpenter without a hammer, or a baker without an oven. The usual response is to seize the nearest method or theory, and pretend to believe it and know how to use it. As a result, the emerging therapist tends to become committed prematurely to imperfectly understood methods and theories. There are several principles, however, which can set a tone for growth and change and which transcend specific theoretical issues. We will list some and encourage you to try them.

EVERYONE CAN CHANGE.   This may not be so, regarding the given therapist and the given patient. However, to be optimally helpful, the therapist must proceed with each patient, no matter how poor "the prognosis," *as if* it were so. It is necessary to remind oneself of this with difficult and resistant patients.

ACCEPTANCE.   "Nothing about ourselves can be changed until it is first accepted" (Kopp, 1970, p. 78). Acceptance is a key issue in therapy, and constitutes the basic attitude each therapist must project. Accepting others and accepting oneself are the most important traits every patient must examine and develop.

HONESTY.   Practically every patient will view the therapist with a combination of blind trust and suspicion. To counter this distortion and to avoid the tempting pitfalls of saying expedient things that may seem initially helpful (e.g., false praise to build ego strength), always be honest. Do not be afraid to occasionally criticize or voice concern and disagreement. If emotional support is endlessly and indiscriminately given, it can become meaningless and suspect. Be aware that the patient may sense your real feelings and intentions. The chances of helping are then greatly reduced; or worse, we unknowingly enter into a conspiracy to maintain the status quo.

RESISTANCE.   Knowing or sensing the therapist's weaknesses, most patients will try to exploit them in order to keep from changing. Remember always that a significant part of the patient's character does not want to change, even when the patient knows that change would be in his best interest. Effective therapy requires a tenacious effort by the clinician to implement change. Take care that this goal never deteriorates into a power struggle or contest since the most destructive behavior can stem from the healthy desire to survive and protect one's integrity. Rather identify with the struggle and expose the healthy core. Avoid playing the role of the adversary, or the idol; both lead to stalemate.

In keeping with the active mode of therapy that we have recommended throughout, the next step in considering behavior change is to recognize that all psychotherapy is, to some degree, behavior modification. As Chessick (1969, p. 76) notes:

> If we face the fact that we *always* are conditioning the thought and behavior of our patients, whether we like it or not, it becomes vital to examine the ways in which this can be done and bring it under more conscious scrutiny.

The ways in which we modify behavior are too numerous to mention. Every gesture, verbalization, inflection, posture, and look conveys expectations and judgments. The early psychoanalysts' attempt to control these influences by making the therapist a neutral and aloof figure was understandable, but eventually futile. We suggest again that rather than run from these influences, use them in a direct and constructive way.

In presenting a model of acceptance, openness, flexibility, and honesty, the therapist displays traits with which the patient can imitate and identify. Even though the patient may contradict or rebel against these traits, the projection of a consistent model will be inherently therapeutic. As the practitioner elicits desires for constructive change from the patient, and helps clarify the patient's goals, it is appropriate to offer direct suggestions and encouragement to try out those goals. The best way to change behavior is to practice the desired changes; begin with a simple and limited attempt and work up to more complex and encompassing attempts. For example, if a person wants to become more self-assertive in every aspect of his life, encourage him to make a daily or weekly attempt at asserting himself with his wife by expressing a heretofore suppressed opinion. As he becomes confident and successful in this limited trial, then encourage him to follow this pattern of assertiveness with a parent, then with a friend, co-worker, and boss. As each situation reenforces confidence, suggest that the frequency of the instances of self-assertion be increased, and the circumstances broadened. Often the patient sees only the end result and wishes to skip the hard work in between. But living is not a product, it is always a process. Practicing changes is a method whereby the therapist helps to breakdown the task into a series of steps which can be practiced gradually one at a time. In this way, the issues that each individual has difficulty with can be isolated and studied. New approaches can be developed and the patient can, at his own pace, learn to cope with and overcome those resistances which prevent the desired changes.

The authors believe that much of what is called mental health has to do with having a realistic and proven sense of ego mastery, a sense of confidence and personal security which leads to the belief that one can have a meaningful and positive effect on the world. This sense of security and emotional power also recognizes and accepts the reality that some things cannot be changed or influenced, or at least understands the relative costs and benefits of attempts to change the unchangeable.

To help the patient gain this psychological mastery is an obvious therapeutic goal. But more than that, it can be a clear and simple construct around which to build a treatment plan. For example, the clinician begins with developing a body of information about where the patient is now and some idea of how he got to that point. Then, the two develop together some general idea of what the patient wants to attain, both emotionally and behaviorally. In step-by-step manner, tailored to the individual, the psychotherapist seeks to assist each individual through the struggle; to challenge those issues in his life which stifle, sabotage, and frighten away a positive sense of self.

Throughout this process, the therapist must continually prepare, encourage, support, and help evaluate the outcomes. Much of the negative and destructive behavior evidenced in therapy usually reflects an angry striking out from frustration, a frustration that grows from the lack of such mastery. In some cases where ego functioning and reality testing are extremely weak, this step-by-step behavioral approach may not be indicated, but in the authors' experience, this caution is rarely needed.

As the patient progresses, always be alert for the signs of growth, however slight and point them out. Often the patient will not notice positive changes or wait for you to notice them: do so! It is crucial and mandatory that the therapist give balanced, objective, and matter-of-fact evidence of positive growth. However, comments on progress should never be made in a flowery or exaggerated fashion. If your observations are not believable, realistic, and appropriate, they are worse than no encouragement at all. By enumerating the signs of change, the therapist helps the patient develop the ability to judge and evaluate his own improvement. The typical positive changes may include lessened anxiety, reduced somatic symptoms, more relaxed physical bearing, better relations with others, improved rapport and a working alliance with the clinician, and increased ability to face and cope with stressful life circumstances. Most important, when changes occur, the therapist should not only point them out, but should contrast them to the patient's previous behavior. This technique is most effective in demonstrating to the patient the degree of behavioral change, since it provides an objective basis of comparison that cannot be minimized or doubted by the patient.

In summary, never be reluctant to repeat and clarify ideas again and again. Working through is a complex task that requires the building of a strong base of trust and understanding. Be clear, direct, and offer simple suggestions. Let the patient elaborate within a therapeutic framework that has firmly established the basics.

Probably the best advice the authors can offer in dealing with changing behavior is to strive for focus. Periodically, review the progress that has been made and set about redefining (or reaffirming) your mutual goals. Sailing continually through uncharted seas, you must pause from time to time to check your compass and consult the charts to see where you have been, make sure you know where you are, and reconfirm where you are headed.

Chapter 7

TERMINATING AND EVALUATING THERAPY

When to consider terminating therapy is one of the most bothersome issues that confronts the neophyte therapist. Even experienced therapists often have difficulty in deciding when and how termination should take place. This problem results from a number of factors, operating alone or in combination, which every therapist must evaluate and keep in mind.

First, a specific contract should have been established between therapist and patient that posited well-defined goals capable of being evaluated by the patient's changed behavior. If either the therapist or patient is hazy about why therapy was initiated and what the patient wants and needs help with (e.g., fear of sexual involvement, aggression toward others, inability to make and hold friends, etc.), treatment will then continue in a fuzzy and meandering manner. This lack of clarity can result in one of the greatest therapeutic "sins": a lack of focus that generates a never-ending therapeutic relationship.

Second, problems in terminating may reflect the clinician's need to feel omnipotent, and to believe that psychotherapy can and should resolve every troublesome or conflict-ridden life situation. Although related to a poorly-defined contract, this issue deserves special mention. All therapists are prone to the belief that they can solve most, perhaps all, problems presented by patients. Therapists can easily develop a "rescue" or "hero" fantasy: the therapist is the hero who will rescue the patient from all his suffering and problems. Although it is important that the therapist be confident that he can help the patient, this positive therapeutic outlook must be tempered with humility and reality. Psychotherapy is not the panacea for an individual's problems and each therapist must come to terms with that fact. Furthermore, to view each patient's problems as a challenge that must be totally overcome and solved can cause the therapist to impose his need to be omnipotent on the outcome of therapy. Imposing this value, to heal completely, on the therapeutic relationship can also make therapy an artificial and endless encounter. Keeping in mind the Greek maxim, "All passes into mystery," is a forceful reminder that life can never be fully understood.

A third factor that can hinder and confuse the termination process arises from the universal desire to have someone to talk to and depend upon. Nearly everyone seeks advice and looks for solutions. Witness the best seller lists with their preponderance of "how to" books that guarantee everything from peace of mind to financial success and sexual perfection. Perhaps the deepest human need is to find a magic solution that will cure all troubles and cares. The dependency of childhood dies hard in all of us. And when one finds a person, like a therapist, who is sympathetic and ready to listen, the need to remain dependent can create obstacles to ending therapy. Therapists can easily become a crutch; the good, all-powerful parent from whom the patient resists separating. Conversely, this situation may also hold for the therapist who may become dependent on the patient for many types of gratification. This dependency may reflect needs for adulation, superiority, and omnipotence. The type and intensity of the symbiotic relationship between therapist and patient requires constant evaluation and self-awareness especially when therapy enters its final phase.

A fourth reason that may delay or prevent an appropriate termination relates to the therapist's anxiety about losing income. When a therapist's hours are dwindling, it is often easy for the therapist to rationalize that a patient needs more therapy. Similarly, when therapy hours are filled, and additional patients are referred, the therapist may be more ready to terminate and begin a "new challenge."

These constitute the primary conditions, which exist to varying degrees of self-awareness, that operate to influence the manner in which the termination process is handled by the therapist. It is the therapist's responsibility to remain ever cognizant of these influences so that an effective termination phase is set in motion.

INDICATIONS FOR ENDING TREATMENT

When should therapy end and how does the therapist recognize that termination is near? The most obvious time for considering termination arrives when the major initial complaints and conflicts reported originally by the patient have been alleviated significantly and no longer exist or cause distress. This answer does not apply to the conflicts and problems that become uncovered as therapy evolves, and which the patient may see as new areas for resolution. We believe, however, that when the terms of the initial therapeutic contract are being met (e.g., overcoming fear of making friends, controlling aggression, achieving sexual adequacy, etc.) the therapist must make the patient aware that the agreed-upon goals are being or have been accomplished. This enables both to evaluate where therapy is at, and whether there is any need to work on another conflict area that has been disclosed or experienced by the patient as requiring further therapeutic intervention.

The overriding criteria for terminating therapy is the patient's improved functioning, sense of well-being, freedom from the distress which caused him to seek therapy and the patient's belief and feeling that he can confidently cope with situations that previously impaired his functioning. This view recognizes that termination evolves from the patient and is not imposed by the therapist. As therapists we should both accept and encourage the patient's sense of progress. Although it may be obvious that some basic conflicts still exist, the therapist must be careful not to minimize a patient's perceived improvement by focusing only on our notion of "the work still to be done." The beginning therapist often defines successful therapy as one that has resolved *all* the underlying and primary conflicts. Theoretically, this is the ideal result which seldom happens. If termination is approached from that point of view, we will usually overlook real progress and impose our values on the patient.

For example, after 20 months of regular weekly sessions with 32-year-old Ellen, who sought therapy to overcome a crippling phobia about driving and to resolve a three-year love relationship that remained infantile and purposeless, termination was raised when Ellen felt that her basic conflicts and symptoms were being handled and diminishing. Of greatest importance was the fact that Ellen was experiencing more fulfillment and strength, and little of her former tension and anguish. While evaluating her progress Ellen had begun to understand the tremendous infantile dependency needs that existed between her mother and herself. She understood that this need to remain a dependent child was primarily responsible for the fear of driving. Her phobia symbolized a fear of leaving home, venturing into the world, and achieving an independent adult adjustment. Adulthood, with its demand to be self-sufficient, terrified Ellen. Consequently, she decided to become a nun and joined a convent after high school graduation. Ellen left the convent after two years and returned home. She found a job as a receptionist with a local physician who was a close family friend and lived only around the corner. The physician-employer, who became a father figure to Ellen, afforded her the protection and dependency she always sought. Her social life was confined to activities that revolved solely around a large family of many siblings and innumerable relatives. There were no friends or interests beyond the family with one exception: a boy friend, 12 years older than Ellen, who submitted graciously and meekly to her demands. Ellen's entire existence reflected dependency and protection.

When Ellen raised the idea of terminating, many changes in her behavior had occurred. She was aware of the dependency upon her mother and family with its implications of continued childlike and constricted daily functioning. Working on this basic conflict and toward greater self-assertion led to many gradual changes. For the first time in several years, Ellen began driving beyond the small village area to which she had restricted herself. She began to make efforts to develop friends beyond her family. She married (after a year of therapy) and successfully managed her own home. She conquered being terrified of her mother's disapproval and gave up their unhealthy symbiotic relationship. The daily anxiety attacks and panic when alone at home occur now only once or twice a month. At this stage in therapy, Ellen is not completely free of her phobia about driving. Although she can drive 10 to 20 miles from her home, Ellen has still not completely resolved the dependency conflict toward her mother. She evidences, however, significant and continuing signs of growth, and confidently feels that she is in control of the negative influences that generated such immobilizing fear and dependency. Ellen feels stronger, happier, more confident, and able to cope with life; she has overcome the helplessness and dissatisfaction that characterized her former life. Therefore, Ellen wonders how much longer she will be in therapy. Experiencing growing inner strength and freedom, Ellen is ready to be on her own.

Therapy may never be able to do away completely with a person's conflicts, but will significantly improve ways of understanding and coping so that the neurotic or irrational behavior will be minimized and neutralized. When that point is reached, terminating therapy becomes a valid consideration. If the therapist had not acknowledged Ellen's emerging strength and focused on the remaining problems, he may have diminished both his effectiveness and the patient's positive self-perceptions. Ellen's dependency would have probably transferred from the mother to the therapist.

When the patient broaches termination, the therapist should evaluate objectively and honestly with the patient how much therapeutic progress has occurred and how the patient views his growth. If termination is premature, the therapeutic gains could be lost without sufficient time for consolidating progress. Similarly, if therapy continues beyond a point of meaning and need for the patient, therapeutic progress could be harmed. Patients may lose heart and confidence if, after sufficient growth and consolidation, the therapist encourages continued treatment. If one is to err, it should be on the side of the patient. Accepting the patient's need to terminate will usually reenforce his emerging confidence and strength. Disagreeing with his readiness to terminate, on the other hand, can undermine progress and plant seeds of self-doubt. And if the therapist properly handles the termination process, the patient who has terminated prematurely will accept the reality of resuming therapy; whereas, the patient who has continued interminably will resist future help when needed.

In summary, the specifics that must be evaluated when considering the feasibility of ending treatment are:

1. To what degree have the goals of the original therapeutic contract been achieved?
2. Have the subsequent goals, disclosed by ongoing therapy, been achieved?
3. Have the behavior changes or goals persisted for a reasonable amount of time and in a variety of situations?

4. What objectives yet remain to be more fully attained, and is the client currently showing emerging signs of fulfilling the remaining objectives?
5. What is the quality of the patient's behavior? Does the patient experience increased happiness, greater self-fulfullment and a significant alleviation of former distress?

CUES FROM THE PATIENT AND THERAPIST

The actual mechanics of termination should continue to reflect the mutual partnership and working alliance of the therapist and patient with special emphasis on the patient's readiness and ability to handle this new development. Who should raise the question of termination is frequently pondered by the neophyte therapist. More often than not it is a natural process, a rhythmic flow that emerges and sets in motion an awareness in both participants that the terminating phase is near. The crucial issue is for the therapist to be sensitive to his own and the patient's cues, which can be both internal and external at this time. Who actually and directly verbalizes the issue of ending therapy is less important than being aware of those signs which point to termination.

Such cues consist primarily of changes in the patient's productivity, behavior, and attitude. As termination approaches, the patient will have less to discuss and fewer problem areas or conflict issues to raise; perhaps he will begin to talk more about superficialities and engage in chit-chat. An appointment may be missed or arrived at late when this has never happened before. Qualitatively, the patient may evidence a more casual manner and seem less interested or intense during the sessions. Therapy will not be experienced as seriously as before. The patient may start to talk about himself with a positive attitude and begin to relate, even brag, about recent accomplishments. Questions or hints at how much longer therapy will be are more direct indications of the patient's growth and progress. The patient's attitude toward the therapist may reveal subtle changes such as acting with less awe and greater freedom. Consequently there may be a reaching out to know the therapist as a person. The therapist will be talked to and related to more as a friend and peer, rather than as an expert or powerful authority figure. When these signs emerge, singly or in combination, within the context of demonstrably improved behavior (i.e., the goals of the therapeutic contract are being achieved), conditions then exist to consider termination. It goes without saying that the therapist must be constantly aware of and attuned to indications of resistance in the patient. Obviously, some of the foregoing cues and reactions can be signs of resistance, rather than of therapeutic growth. The major criterion that differentiates between resistance and signs of therapeutic progress, which presages terminating therapy, always derives from evaluating the therapeutic contract: Are the goals of therapy being achieved as evidenced by the patient's behavior? The answer to this question of how much therapeutic progress has been made, in accordance with the contract of therapy, will indicate clearly whether the patient is resisting or informing you that he is ready to consider concluding treatment.

Just as cues come from the patient, there are also cues coming from the therapist which indicate that the termination phase is approaching. To illustrate, the therapist may find that he is becoming increasingly aware of the patient's improved behavior and is beginning to ponder how many more therapeutic gains yet need to be evidenced. The therapist may subtly begin to prepare less for therapy sessions than when the patient's problems were unresolved and rife. As with the patient when termination is in the offing, the therapist may also feel more relaxed and casual, and act less intensely and seriously because of the implicit or explicit realization that therapeutic gains are being made and sustained. Moreover, the therapist may unconsciously manifest his diminished anxiety and greater confidence in the patient by cancelling or being late for a session, or even forgetting the time of the patient's sessions. Lastly, the therapist's sense of success and accomplishment will provide another important influence for broaching termination. When one or more of these signs are experienced by the therapist within the context of the patient's improved functioning and accompanied with evidence that the therapeutic goals are being achieved, the therapist can conclude that the need for termination is at hand.

METHODS OF TERMINATION

Ending therapy, like any other therapeutic stage or development, should always reflect the fact that effective psychotherapy is a partnership, a mutuality of effort. Motivated by that belief, the termination process should reflect, to a greater or lesser degree, a course of action which has been arrived at and agreed to by both patient and therapist. The therapist should therefore present the various options open to the patient to effect termination. We believe that concluding therapy can proceed in one of three ways:

1. The patient and therapist should arrive at an agreed upon termination date that allows for a review and consolidation of gains. This date can vary from two weeks to several months from the moment that the idea of termination is raised. If the evaluation of therapeutic progress reveals major and persistent changes, we usually find that therapy can terminate within two to eight weeks. An immediate or abrupt termination with no chance for discussion, review, and preparation will indicate unresolved difficulties in the therapist–patient relationship, or, in psychoanalytic terms, a negative transference that has not adequately been

dealt with by the therapist. Although intense external or environmental pressures (e.g., a spouse's pressures, financial losses) may be brought upon the patient to terminate therapy, an abrupt termination still shows that the patient has problems in relating effectively to the therapist since he is ready to submit to these pressures without discussing them thoroughly. In circumstances where the patient's growth is at a plateau or standstill and significant goals still need to be attained, establishing a fixed termination several months distant may be agreed upon. This termination arrangement can be highly effective and therapeutic since it can mobilize the patient (and therapist) to work harder during therapy sessions. In his article on terminating psychoanalysis, Freud (1924) noted by telling his patient that the coming year was to be the last year of analysis, the patient became sufficiently mobilized to move away from his resistances and make significant therapetuic progress. On the other hand, patients who have shown sufficient progress and set a termination date too far distant are communicating an ambivalence about separating from the therapist and/or a need to continue therapy because of still unresolved problems. If the latter holds true, the therapist is being told that he needs to work yet more intensely with the patient.

2. Another option for terminating consists of a gradual phasing out with a fixed time set for concluding therapy. The decision can be made to have biweekly rather than regular once-a-week therapy sessions. This arrangement enables the patient to separate gradually from therapy. alternate weekly therapy sessions also afford the patient longer periods of time between therapy to evaluate and test out therapeutic progress and gains.

3. The last option is to offer alternate weekly sessions within an open-ended framework, or with no definite target date for termination. This plan should be presented with the understanding that the patient can gradually decrease the frequency of visits to once every three or four weeks, or in accordance with the patient's needs and progress. The patient who decides upon this type of termination still needs the security and a structure that is minimally demanding and maximally designed to terminate at his own rate. However, at some time period in this arrangement a termination date should be established so that therapy does not proceed indefinitely.

The method of termination chosen should, as already noted, reflect agreement between the patient and the therapist. Many factors will influence the termination plan, but the most important are 1) the patient's own perceptions and feelings about his therapeutic gains and readiness to go it alone, and 2) the therapist's evaluation of the patient's behavioral changes, especially those reflecting greater personal integration, self-fulfillment, and increased responsibility. Both patient and therapist must feel comfortable with the termination method and substantially agree about what has been achieved and the problems which still may need therapeutic work or are on their way to resolution. Adopting one or another termination plan will also be determined by the extent of the patient's dependency on therapy and the patient's own rhythm or style in effecting change and independent action. However, the therapist must be constantly on guard to ferret out resistances to change (i.e., termination), and to avoid giving in to the patient's dependency needs by prolonging treatment. Usually, patients who are genuinely ready to end therapy will decide on a termination plan fairly quickly, decisively, and with a rationale harmonious with their personality style and needs.

Preparing the Patient for Termination

In addition to agreeing upon a definite plan for termination, there are some important considerations to be aware of during this concluding phase of therapy. With regard to the date of termination, the therapist should strictly adhere to the agreed upon time for discontinuing therapy. We believe that to break this agreement and extend therapy could cause the patient to lose faith and confidence in the therapist. Besides, the patient could begin to question his progress and to doubt himself, thereby impairing some of the therapeutic accomplishments. We recognize, however, that flexibility may need to prevail; a situation (e.g., an illness) may arise that will have to extend the fixed termination date by a week or two. Similarly, the patient may be experiencing such strength and eagerness to be on his own that he may request that termination be moved up a week or more. In this situation, the therapist should go along with the patient and support his desire to end therapy slightly sooner than initially planned. The therapist's support at this time can be very crucial in maximizing and accelerating the patient's self-confidence and inner strength. Indulging in unnecessary questions and overanalyzing the patient's request for earlier termination can undermine the patient's growth and faith in the therapist.

Still another important factor, during the termination process, concerns preparing the patient for life without therapy. The therapist should reassure the patient that he will experience intermittent periods of self-doubt, anxiety about having ended therapy too soon, and perhaps flashes of former ineffective reactions to life situations, and that these are natural feelings that do not lessen the growth and progress made in therapy. The phenomenon of "termination regression" or the brief return of old symptoms during and shortly after the termination process is not uncommon. Preparing the patient for these probable negative reactions will help combat and minimize anxieties and doubts that stem from being separated from therapy. The patient should also be told that he can always call or return for a therapy session if and when he feels the need for further help. By acknowledging that situations may occur that may require a future call or visit reassures the patient that he can seek your help without feeling embarrassed. It is important to convey that recurring or new problems do not necessarily represent a failure on the patient's part and should not be viewed by the patient as a return to his former maladjusted reactions. Like every human being, the patient must be helped to accept the fact that no one is perfect, and that no one can always solve or cope well with conflicts. Stresses and crises arise periodically to cause everyone to lapse into irrational and ineffective ways of reacting and coping, but this does not signify that we are failures. Emphasizing this fact during termination helps the patient fight the tendency to feel that he is weak and a failure when confronted by a future crisis. Besides, this preparation and reassurance will also combat the patient's inclination to believe his therapeutic progress and gains have been false.

UNSUCCESSFUL TERMINATION

This entire discussion and focus on termination has only concerned itself with the successful patient. Nothing has been said about patients whose therapy is a failure or, at best, minimally effective. Every therapist will work with patients who cannot be helped, or at least not helped by you, the present therapist. As therapists, we must realize and accept the fact that we cannot be effective and successful with all patients and all types of problems. It therefore behooves us to arrive at an understanding of the kind of patients and problems with which we experience little or no success. This knowledge should influence the kind of goals set forth in the contract by limiting and qualifying our expectations, and by making us aware that we may require additional supervision while working with such a patient. Difficult patients should also mobilize us to greater effort. Moreover, this awareness of our limitations with a particular patient should make us pause and question whether we should take this type of patient on for therapy. It is often more advisable and judicious to refer patients with whom we have had little success in the past to another psychotherapist. The effective therapist is the professional who also knows his limitations and weaknesses.

An appropriate illustration concerns Dr. B., a 30-year-old therapist of a few years' therapeutic experience, who could not cope with the manipulative, provocative, and resistant behavior of Mrs. P., a 48-year-old divorced patient. She would call the therapist at all hours of the day to bemoan her existence, suddenly cancel appointments, and constantly try to provoke during sessions by attacking and questioning his competence. During supervision we found that Dr. B had never truly achieved, after many months of therapy, an effective relationship with her. Rapport was poor and the transference reflected much ambivalence and negativism. In exploring his feelings and reactions to Mrs. P., Dr. B. discovered that she reminded him of his domineering mother who always found fault with him and questioned his every action. To cope with this attacking and disapproving mother, Dr. B. adopted a passive and withdrawn defensive stance. He would lapse into silences and avoid involvement with her. Dr. B. soon realized the countertransference problem with Mrs. P. He began to see how his needs as a son and man to attack or defend himself from his mother (patient) alternated with the need to be an understanding and accepting therapist. Thus, his reactions toward Mrs. P. ranged from passivity to sympathy to open hostility. During Mrs. P.'s verbal attacks and cries for acceptance, Dr. B. vacillated between silences, detachment, and withdrawal to blunt exhortations and verbal counterattacks. This negative countertransference became further complicated by Dr. B.'s periods of understanding, patience, and reassurances toward Mrs. P. No wonder Mrs. P. did not move from her position of resistance;

she did not feel safe with her therapist who was quite inconsistent and erratic. These insights helped Dr. B further understand previous therapeutic difficulties he had been experiencing periodically with older, domineering and aggressive female patients. Accordingly, Dr. B. began, in supervision, to work through this problem of handling the intense unconscious resentment and anger toward female patients who displayed the controlling and fault-finding behavior of his overly critical mother. This knowledge provided Dr. B. with the understanding to implement more consistent and effective techniques in working with this type of patient. Incidentally, Dr. B. terminated with Mrs. P. who had started to question him about the advisability of working with an "older and more mature therapist." Furthermore, Dr. B. decided against taking on any new older female patients until he resolved this problem of being threatened and uncomfortable with those who exhibited the personality style of his disapproving mother.

When therapeutic failure seems imminent, the therapist must quickly evaluate the situation and make a decision to terminate or continue therapy. If the therapeutic relationship remains ineffective and is characterized by resistance, and if no therapeutic gains are seen or felt, therapy should be terminated. If the therapist procrastinates at this point, therapy can deteriorate into a pointless and painful exercise. Most important, the patient can be discouraged and more resistant to seeking aid from another therapist who could provide the help you were not able to give. The most effective way to handle this matter of a therapuetic impasse and failure is to inform the patient of your belief that an effective and workable therapeutic relationship has not developed. (It is understood that this is expressed only after your efforts to resolve the resistance have failed.) Therefore, you recommend that therapy should terminate and present the reasons for this belief. The therapist must be cautious to avoid acting antagonistically and disrespectfully toward the patient at this crucial time. He should explain the recommendation openly and honestly so that the patient is not denigrated. Is is also important to present your explanations in such a manner that the patient can still feel hopeful about receiving psychotherapy from someone else. You should do whatever you can to prepare the patient to seek therapy with another therapist, although the negative and ambivalent atmosphere which brought on this situation may undermine these future efforts. Usually, at this time, the patient will be aware of the lack of therapeutic success and be ready to accept the recommendation to terminate. Not infrequently, the patient may raise the issue before you do so that termination will seem to emerge or flow naturally from the situation.

When this impasse is openly discussed, there is always the possibility that both the patient and therapist will become sufficiently mobilized and challenged to resolve this failure, and develop a more effective working relationship that leads to ultimate therapeutic success.

Chapter 8

PERFECTING YOUR THERAPEUTIC SKILLS

It is amazing how little, if anything, is taught during formal professional training of psychotherapy about the importance of developing and refining one's skills as a therapist. Like any craft, psychotherapy requires constant practice, learning, and refinement. Just as an artist needs to practice and learn new musical scores, the psychotherapist must perpetually practice and review his knowledge and techniques. As the artist grows and matures, his artistic skills and interpretations will change: the pianist's Chopin prelude, the painter's water lilies, and the writer's slice-of-life will each be rendered differently at different times of the artist's life. This phenomenon illustrates that the individual's craft as well as his life is not static, but always evolving or in a state of flux. The artist who does not grow, who continues to interpret the world and his art in the same old way, who does not venture forth and try new things will stagnate, become ineffective, and lose his audience. Compare Beethoven's early and late chamber music, Dostoevsky's beginning essays and the last great novels, Picasso's early paintings and his later changing styles and output which ranged widely to every form of graphic arts.

We emphasize the importance of personal growth and evolvement because its acceptance and recognition is crucial to one's development as an effective psychotherapist. If after years of practicing, your psychotherapeutic skills and knowledge have not developed beyond what was learned during formal training, your therapeutic effectiveness and proficiency will remain seriously limited. Perhaps one of the greatest modern day examples of professional growth is Karl Menninger who celebrated his 85th birthday in 1977. In over 50 years as a mental health practitioner, Dr. Menninger, one of the earliest psychoanalysts in America, has applied and extended his knowledge and skills to nearly every aspect of mental health treatment. Upon receiving the American Psychiatric Association's first Founder's Award in 1977, Dr. Menninger continued to challenge all of us to grow when he said, "But I want you to think, while you are treating these patients, what further knowledge we ought to have in order to treat them better" (Robbins & Herman, p. 305, 1978). To find this "further knowledge" is the ever present obligation and challenge of the psychotherapist. And one of the major approaches to such further knowledge is through developing and refining one's own skills. Suggestions toward achieving this goal will be outlined below. The authors must, however, preface these recommendations by stating that they do not exhaust the ways of maximizing professional growth, since growth is only limited by the individual's desire, daring, ingenuity, creativity, and willingness to work hard.

TRAINING AND PROFESSIONAL AFFILIATIONS

We deplore the many growing off-shoots in our society and educational system today that purport to train psychotherapists without proper accreditation by one of the mental health professions. Witness the many programs and courses in the self-help and encounter movements that promise to make you a psychotherapist in several weeks or months. The psychotherapists to whom these guidelines are addressed comprise those who are still in training or have graduated from a recognized educational institution. Although formal professional training stops at some point, training and learning one's craft should never end. An effective way to continue informal training consists of joining national, regional, and/or local professional organizations that keep you aware of professional matters. Most important, belonging to professional associations provide the psychotherapist with a sense of identity with a profession, a feeling that can be lost or weakened in the lonely atmosphere of private practice. Meeting and being with colleagues to discuss common issues and experiences is crucial in combating the sense of loneliness and isolation from the professional community that can easily occur in private practice. Similarly, one should plan to regularly attend meetings such as conventions, workshops, seminars, and special lectures to keep abreast of theoretical and practical issues, as well as to be aware of how one's profession reflects and affects the broader cultural mores of the times. To be ignorant of how society has been and is influenced by psychotherapeutic ideas and techniques will impair one's understanding of the individual and the world in which he lives.

READING

Reading must be actively cultivated and pursued if we hope to truly begin to understand ourselves and our civilization. Such understanding is essential in aiding us to accept and appreciate our patients' problems. Every psychotherapist should regularly read at least several professional journals and as many books as possible each year in his psychotherapeutic specialty. A reading approach that we find very fruitful in learning new concepts or perfecting a technique is to concentrate on one article or book at a time, and return to it repeatedly. This method not only gets you to focus on the ideas you want to learn, but enables you to review and refresh your thinking about a specific topic of study. With the voluminous barrage of books and articles that bombard us today, this approach can be most helpful to the beginning psychotherapist. For example, we recently advised during supervision of a therapist, who does not yet feel comfortable and proficient with her initial interview techniques, to read and study Harry Stack Sullivan's classic, *The Psychiatric Interview* (1954). The essential points are to focus on only one book for a period of time until you grasp the concepts and techniques in which you are interested, and to pick a book that reflects your own theoretical beliefs. Once a particular book's viewpoints have been understood and mastered, go on to other presentations that offer varying views. Even experienced therapists should consider cultivating this habit of studying a single book to review and refresh ideas and techniques. Books that have greatly influenced the authors' own professional and personal growth, and which we return to regularly include: the aforementioned H. S. Sullivan, Angyal's *Neurosis and Treatment* (1965), Chessick's *How Psychotherapy Heals* (1969), Freud's *Collected Papers* (1950), Fromm-Reichman's *Principles of Intensive Psychotherapy* (1950), and *Therapeutic Communication* by Jurgen Reusch (1961).

Perhaps just as important as reading professional topics is reading the world's literature. Novelists, biographers, and poets can teach us more about the human condition, its complexities, and motivations, than any number of professional texts. Who can show us a greater portrait of death and suffering than Tolstoy's Ivan Ilyich, of the anguish of contemporary life described in Cheever, Updike, and Bellow, of the obsessive need to prove one's mastery in Hemingway's heros, of how social changes affect the individual in Chekhov's protagonists, and of how mankind suffers and endures in Greek tragedies and the

Bible. The great writers since time immemorial have been master psychologists and teachers.

This combination of training, professional affiliations, and continuous reading is basic to being attuned to professional developments and life around us. Without these foundations how would we learn and know of the many changes evidenced in the past few generations such as the evolving psychoanalytic techniques that now stress ego functions; the emergence of Gestalt group and encounter techniques that also recognize the importance of physical (bodily) expression and relaxation; the principle of biofeedback and the growing recognition of physiological conditioning in pain, stress, and psychosomatic conditions; the sexual revolution with its proliferating effects on the roles of men and women, abortion, women's rights, and homosexuality; the return to behavioral therapies that stress learning and conditioning principles in more refined and ingenious ways; and finally, the rise of individual rights and its enormous influences on race, religion, and government. Every psychotherapist who counsels and works with troubled people must be aware of all such professional and societal developments if he wants to help the patient to the best of his professional responsibility.

SUPERVISION

The next or third course of action in learning the actual day-to-day practice of therapy and refining therapeutic skills is obtaining supervision, which should be mandatory. By supervision we refer to the process of regularly meeting with a senior and experienced clinician to discuss the problems and concerns that the patient arouses in you the therapist. The term "control therapist" or "control analyst" is usually used to describe this type of supervision which should provide a constructive, critical review of the therapist's diagnostic understanding of the patient and therapeutic strategy. Supervision offers a method that enables the psychotherapist to discuss his doubts, anxieties, and puzzlement over a patient and provides feedback, advice, and ideas from a more experienced and knowledgeable clinician. Inherent in the supervisory process is the opportunity for the control therapist to point out the supervisee's strengths and weaknesses as a therapist. From supervision you will learn the type of patients that will touch on your own neurotic conflicts and the type of reactions they set off in you, i.e., the transference and countertransference that exists. Recently during supervision with Dr. Jean, a clincial psychologist intern, we observed that her inability to relate and work effectively with middle-aged men with marital problems stemmed from the resentment and vindictiveness she harbored toward her father and her ex-husband. When she worked with passive, dependent, and ineffectual men, Dr. Jean displaced annoyance and anger onto them because such male patients called to mind the same characteristics of a father and a husband who failed and hurt her. This observation may seem obvious and elementary, but it took many sessions and repeated discussions to aid Dr. Jean in realizing this negative countertransference and its effects. This example also shows that during ongoing supervision, the control therapist may explore your own background and feelings about a patient in order to evaluate your interaction with the patient.

The nature of the therapeutic interaction and how it affects therapy probably constitutes the most important facts that can be derived from supervision. At this point, it should be noted that supervision can be approached by the supervisor in one of three ways:

1. focusing solely on the patient with the emphasis placed on clarifying the diagnosis, dynamics, and recommending therapeutic strategy.
2. concentrating primarily on the therapist's feelings and ideas about the patient, with the emphasis directed on clarifying the transference/countertransference relationship, or the therapist–patient interaction.

3. a combination of both of these approaches, which the
    authors recommend.

Whatever approach is used in supervision, the major goals
should always be to arrive at a better understanding of the
patient and to recommend therapeutic techniques that will enhance therapeutic proficiency. Supervision, therefore, helps to
develop objectivity and avoid the pitfalls of uncontrolled sub-
jectivity. And to achieve this dual goal from supervision, the
therapist must feel comfortable with and accepted by the supervisor. If threatened, intimidated, and patronized by the control
therapist, the practitioner should seek other supervision. Incidentally, supervision is something that can be contracted for
unless provided as a requirement within a clinic, hospital, or
other organizational setting. In the latter case, the matter of
choice is usually not given. Therefore, it is important that the
theoretical and experiential background of the supervision be
recognized and understood. Such awareness will enable the
therapist to take from supervision the things most consistent
and harmonious with his therapeutic and personal goals. We
always recall the emphasis that our control analyst, Dr. David
Gross,* made repeatedly: listen to my recommendations and
evaluations, but take from them only what makes sense to you
and, most importantly, implement them in your own individual
style; furthermore, learn to follow your feelings.

A supervising theapist should have a theoretical background and personality style that is congenial and similar to
your therapeutic training and philosophy so that professional
growth is maximized. For example, it would make little sense
to seek supervision from an analytically trained therapist if you
were trained in behavior modification techniques, unless you
specifically wanted to learn other theoretical and different ther-

---

*The senior author will always remember and be grateful to the late
David Gross, M.D., New York City, a training analyst for Willian Alanson
White Institute, who provided not only invaluable clinical knowledge, but a
model of professional excellence.

apeutic tasks than your own. We also stress the importance of having a "role model," a mentor whom you can admire and learn from without reservation, if you can be so fortunate. There is no greater aid, excitement, and desire to learning than to find and become associated with a teacher you admire and respect not only for his knowledge and skills, but also for his approach to work and life. There is no more effective way to learn a therapeutic philosophy and technique than by copying the things you see from an admired and successful clinician and teacher. But follow one cautionary principle: what you take from your teacher must always be adapted and interpreted according to your own personal style. The knowledge and skills copied must be adapted in a flexible and creative fashion and not be just a slavish and rigid imitation of what is being taught. Just as you try to emulate the tennis professional's smooth and relaxed backhand, try to imitate the clinician whom you see as a model, knowing always that the learning must be integrated according to your own needs, limitations, and strengths. Especially in this day of fierce educational competition, huge teaching loads, and impersonal teaching, it becomes even more important to find a mentor from whom you can learn in this highly individual fashion of supervision. And if such a model cannot be found, search the world of literature for a model. When you read an author who strikes a responsive chord in you (that "shock of recognition"), read more of his works and concentrate on his teachings. For example, we have had that reaction to the works of Harry Stack Sullivan and over the years have continued to learn from his writings, which never fail to impress with his sense of humor, wit, gentleness, curiosity, respect for patients, profound empathy, and sense of humility that pervade and illuminate his clinical approach.

Throughout this chapter, the emphasis has been on professional development and growth as an evolving and ongoing process. Similarly, supervision is, to some extent, a never-ending process. No matter how well trained and experienced, every clinician needs supervision or the opportunity to periodically review cases with a colleague(s) for advice regarding therapeutic strategy. How long regular formal supervision should be sought depends on individual needs and training. During the first 10 years of private practice, one of the authors saw his control therapist biweekly for two-hour sessions. And now he tries to maintain an approach that will readily seek out advice and reactions from other colleagues whenever certain patients present difficulties for us. No one is too experienced to learn from a supervisor or a colleague. The excitement and challenge of psychotherapy is the ever-present emergence of a new problem that confronts the therapist for the first time: the first time you work with a phobia, a suicide, an imminent psychotic break, or a compulsive reaction. We can all remember those "first times" when we floundered and sought knowledge and advice from supervision. Finally, we must acknowledge and confess that the supervisor, too, receives a form of supervision from those clinicians whom he trains and supervises. Not only do those seeking supervision demand and force the teacher to keep on top of his form, but, more importantly, they provide an endless source of new information, varying viewpoints, and different needs which challenge and test the supervisor's knowledge and skills. What better way to grow and perfect therapeutic skills than from such a constant challenge?

PSYCHOTHERAPY FOR PSYCHOTHERAPISTS?

The matter of personal psychotherapy for the beginning psychotherapist must now be considered. The authors wholeheartedly endorse and recommend psychotherapy for the emerging clinician. The overriding importance of such therapy is to help the future therapist become aware of his neurotic conflicts, emotional vulnerabilities, and strengths. It is axiomatic that better self-knowledge and learning to cope with your own problems will contribute to greater effectiveness as a therapist. Moreover, being a patient yourself helps to understand the flavor of therapy and appreciate what patients experience: the fears and uncertainty, the threats of feeling exposed and made vulnerable, the resistances and inhibitions, the satisfactions of new insights, the spurts of growth, change, and self-fulfillment.

If the future clinician is someone who has achieved a fairly mature and well-integrated adjustment relatively free from conflicts then personal psychotherapy may not be essential. But there are few of us so fortunate. As human beings, we all suffer from and are plagued by psychic frailties. And those of us who aspire to keep our psychic house in order should be aware of personal conflicts and their effects on us and others.

We recall one beginning therapist, Dr. Cecily, who tended to be overprotective toward adolescents and young adult patients, and engendered marked dependency feelings in them. Dr. Cecily's own psychotherapy revealed that as a reaction against her own mother's domination and deep resentment of such maternal control, Dr. Cecily needed to feel important and powerful by setting herself up as an omniscient parental figure to these young patients; also, that she was a better parent than her mother. As a consequence of this conflict, Dr. Cecily would ultimately cause these teenagers to resist therapy, or become overdependent. In her own therapy, Dr. Cecily became aware of this conflict and saw how it impaired her therapeutic effectiveness. As a sidelight, Dr. Cecily's personal conflict became most evident in working with demanding and manipulative parents. In these situations, she would become engaged in a power struggle, and sought to convince them that her approach was the best way of handling their child's problem.

If psychotherapy is not undertaken, the psychotherapist should plan a long period of supervision from a control therapist who will focus equally on the patient and on the therapist's reactions as outlined above. Psychotherapists who have personality problems and conflicts with others that remain unresolved need to understand and be aware of those difficulties, or suffer the consequences of having their personal problems displaced onto their patients. It would be unrealistic to demand that a therapist has to be free from personal conflict in order to be a proficient therapist. However, we believe that there are levels of therapeutic competence and proficiency which will be affected, to some degree, by the presence of unresolved life problems in the psychotherapist. It is our view that the extent to which a therapist achieves a well-integrated life and overcomes his neurotic conflicts represents the degree to which the therapist will maximize therapeutic efficacy. We all know successful psychotherapists who have blatant personal problems, but we have no first-hand knowledge of how truly effective these therapists are. Perhaps the profession and public only know their success with certain types of patients and rarely, if ever, learn of their ineffectiveness and failures. And, certainly no one knows how much more proficient the personally troubled psychotherapist would be if he were more free of personal problems. The moral of these remarks is that if anyone should "know thyself" and "heal thyself," it should be the psychotherapist. Therefore, consider seriously our suggestion to seek personal psychotherapy, and failing that, enter into a lengthy period of supervision that enables you to better understand patients, and your own countertransference or reactions to all kinds of patients. You may choose to bypass personal psychotherapy, but supervision is a necessary professional obligation.

INTROSPECTION AND SELF-ANALYSIS

Every clinician, like every human being, stands essentially alone in his search for "the good life." The therapist, it could be argued, bears a greater burden than most because his work implicitly demands and requires that he aid another individual in this quest. Consequently, the therapist is usually placed in the false position of providing a cure-all, a solution, a panacea, or the prescription to the good life. In cultivating the habits of introspection and self-analysis, the psychotherapist helps himself maintain the proper objectivity and psychic distance from the innumerable pressures and stresses generated by patients. By introspection, we mean the active habit of thinking and ruminating about your life, with special reference to the patient pressures confronting you. By self-analysis, we refer to the habit of explaining yourself to yourself, or developing the active habit of trying to understand the reasons for your reactions and behavior. The therapist's greatest and most valuable instrument is himself, and introspection and self-analysis offer major tools for understanding and perfecting this instrument. It take courage to constantly scrutinize yourself. But that is the therapist's obligation and avenue to developing humility, integrity, and objectivity. Even though we all fall short of the genius of a Freud, we would do well to emulate his consuming desire to search and analyze his reactions and behavior within clinical and personal situations. Freud's passion to understand life, his patients, and himself are evidenced throughout his writings as he analyzed his dreams, family life, childhood and professional life. As we think about life and analyze our thoughts and behavior, we lay the foundation for personal growth and the beginning of wisdom, attributes that therapists sorely need in understanding, accepting, and helping others. More importantly, this questioning and analytical attitude will provide answers to the eternal quest for meaning. As you understand yourself and your world more fully, your life can achieve the sense of purpose and meaning that we all strive for. The therapist who avoids contemplating the vicissitudes of life and his own emotions will never fully appreciate the richness of living, and will remain a rigid and stunted person and professional.

The reader need only consider autobiographical and philosophical literature to understand how introspection and self-analysis leads to wisdom and a greater appreciation of self and others. In Camus' *Notebooks,* the great French writer kept notes of his thoughts on death, war, love, loneliness, and art. These personal thoughts and emotions on a variety of issues show the philosophical and intellectual development of a sensitive artistic mind. The classic *Father and Son* of Edmund Gosse reveals how a father's overwhelming spiritual and intellectual domination influenced nearly every aspect of the writer's adult life. Montaigne's essays, Pascal's *Pensees,* the poetry of Emily Dickinson, all illustrate individual attempts to explain and cope with everything that life has to offer: the bright and beautiful, the depths of darkness and tragedy, the quiet desperation of daily existence, the love and hate of others. As we cultivate the habits of introspection and self-analysis, we will arrive at a better idea of ourselves and others. We will develop our own views, which will evolve with age, of the infinite number of relationships and things that constitute human life: friends, mates, children, parents, and of love, death, and failure. And these evolving ideas and feelings will enhance our humanness, thereby enabling us to be better therapists.

A word of caution, however. There are professionals and scholars who avidly pursue these traits in an intellectual fashion, as if thinking and analyzing life were just another academic exercise and challenge. If introspection and self-analysis do not lead to greater self-awareness, fulfillment, and meaning, no matter how slight, then your efforts have been purely a sterile intellectual task. As Camus (1969, p. 33) noted, the fault of psychology is concentrating on details when "men . . . are seeking and analyzing themselves. To know oneself, one should assert oneself. Psychology is action, not thinking about oneself. We continue to shape our personality all our life. If we knew ourselves perfectly, we should die." The thrill and challenge of introspection and analyzing yourself is in applying its results to change your life. Perhaps the excitement of life is that we can always learn something new that can heighten self-fulfillment and meaning. We urge that you work at integrating self-knowledge into your everyday living.

MATURITY

Mental health practitioners make constant and repeated reference to the concept of maturity, and usually view it as an integral goal of psychotherapy. Yet, maturity is an idea that is seldom defined or discussed at length during professional training, probably because everyone takes this commonplace idea for granted and tacitly assumes that it is easily understood by all. Maturity for many simply means being grown-up and no longer a child, being responsible, and being well-adjusted. Since the achievement of maturity is a basic and crucial condition for perfecting therapeutic skills, as well as for personal growth, we wish to discuss the general criteria that best describe a mature individual. Much of this discussion is adapted from and closely follows Gordon Allport's (1937) outline presented in his classic book on personality.

Three characteristics, which seem fairly universal and necessary, distinguish the mature from the immature person, according to Allport: first, the mature person displays the ability to involve himself in the world and have a variety of interests. Allport terms this trait to make friends, to lose yourself in work and recreation, the "Extension of the Self." This characteristic recognizes that egocentricity, the self-centered view of the world that typified childhood, has given way to a genuine interest and concern for others and the external world. Coincidentally, this attribute becomes central to H. A. Overstreet's (1949) "linkage theory" of maturity: the mature man lives by and through relationships. Both Allport and Overstreet stress that the development of outside interests and relationships manifest themselves in planning and pursuing a life goal. A mature person has something to strive and live for: a meaning, a directionality. Whereas, the hopeless potential suicides, in their aimless searchings and experimentations, reveal that a life without purpose becomes unbearable.

As a second requirement for maturity, Allport posits the notion of "Self-Objectification," or the cultivation of insight and humor. Insight is the ability to live without self-deception, or to know and accept one's failings and strengths. Personal strength and wisdom begin at the point when individual weaknesses are acknowledged. Or, in Disraeli's words: "To be conscious that you are ignorant of the facts is a great step to knowledge." As we objectify ourselves and develop a more detached, and less subjective outlook, we gain the insight that leads to a more accepting and realistic view of the world. Also, the development of a sense of humor proceeds from such self-objectification. The mature individual can laugh at himself and others, and views the world's absurdities with bemusement. The humor of Mark Twain, with its lack of pomp, its honesty, and directness exemplifies a mature mind. With insight we lose our pretensions and can begin to laugh and view the human situation with amusement rather than anger.

The third and final requisite for maturity is a "Unifying Philosophy of Life." Whether verbalized or lived by deeds, the philosophy should be an all-embracing one that develops in accordance with individual needs and values. Whether manifested in thought like that of T. S. Eliot, or evident in action like that of Mahatma Ghandi, the unifying philosophy should pervade behavior and affect how one views himself in the scheme of things. An individual philosophy will reflect highly personal values and needs, and provide a frame of reference for living. It is not synonymous with being right or having the answer to life. It is a personal guideline of values and beliefs that fashions our lives and helps us understand where we stand in the universe. Thus, people may be guided by a religious, artistic, scientific, or intellectual philosophy, to cite only a few of the major values from which man develops, singly or in combination, a unifying explanation of life.

A final, but important word about maturity. Often, the idea of adjustment is used synonomously with maturity. In our view, the mature individual is not necessarily the well-adjusted person. Effecting a satisfactory adjustment can mean accepting the values of society at the expense of sacrificing and betraying your own individuality. Human beings have an enormous capacity to submit, to be followers, to passively accept authority. Unfortunately, many individuals would rather take the easy way and accept and obey without question the prevailing establishment and rules of the day. Such individuals probably make a better "adjustment," but we question their maturity since they have usually submitted to the immaturities of the people around them. Rather that assert themselves and follow their own beliefs and values, these people, like Plato's cave dwellers, shut their eyes and follow the path of self-delusion. This distortion of the truth and evasion of reality is pursued to achieve a goal of security that is essentially shaky and false.

These remarks are not intended to ignore and decry the importance of standards, rules, and regulations that are needed as parameters of reality in any institution and culture. Rather, our plea is for the individual to hold fast to his personal freedom and avoid sacrificing his ideals on the altar of "adjustment." Moreover, our institutions should be judged, as Overstreet (1949, p. 74) implored, "by the extent to which they encourage or discourage maturity in all their members." The single greatest change in Western civilization during the 1960s and 1970s has been the rise of the individual. This recognition of individual rights has led to profound and irreversible changes in man's life and outlook: the increasing consciousness of equality in men and women, the demands of blacks and other minorities, the refusal to let individual rights be denied and violated as witnessed by the resignation of an American president and the emergence of new nations all over the world. To remain fiercely independent, to follow our own drummer, to hear our own voice, to listen to our own heart, while acting responsibly and with respect for others is the epitome of emotional maturity. Such a course, therefore, recognizes that you may be out of tune with others and "unadjusted," but you will be in the good company of people like Christ, Lincoln, Schweitzer, Martin Luther King, Einstein, Churchill, and many others who remained true to themselves.

It is our fervent belief that psychotherapy can help the individual achieve personal integration and integrity, and an increased realization of his potential. If therapy is to have any meaning it is "to expand the domain of personal responsibility, authenticity, and integrity in the life of the patient. It is a process of unification and integration of the personality under the dominance of the responsible, authentic person" (Bloom 1977, p. 335).

EXPERIENCE AND AGING

The functions of growing older and accumulating experience, and its relationship to achieving emotional maturity needs special emphasis. Unfortunately, experience and aging do not automatically lead to maturity. An elderly person may be as immature as a teenager while a young adult may display the maturity of an older individual. Although chronological age is not synonymous with an individual's degree of maturity, we believe that experience and aging can lay the foundation for personal development and wisdom. Like a vintage wine, many can benefit from aging and develop their potential. We need not wholly accept George Bernard Shaw's witticism that the only thing we learn from experience is that we do not learn from experience. Experience can and should be a teacher. To ignore learning from life experiences will limit and impair your understanding of the diverse and infinite number of life situations with which you will be confronted. Our own lives can offer invaluable basic training in understanding life. We need not go so far as Plato's prescription in advising doctors themselves to have the diseases they want to cure; however, to learn from our own personal experiences is a valid principle in appreciating and understanding others.

Each of us, as we grow older, has an infinite number of experiences that represent individual variations on the common human condition. All of us experience childhood, adulthood, love, sex, power struggles, illness, death, tragedy, and success. These actual living situations offer priceless learning opportunities. Innumerable illustrations come to mind. The death of both authors' mothers after lengthy terminal illnesses caused us to think more about death and our own mortality and provided a finer appreciation of the sufferings of others when confronted with a serious illness. Being a parent and having just weathered the teenage years of a son and a daughter have helped us better appreciate the anguish that parents undergo. Moreover, many of our childhood conflicts have taken on a different flavor; for example, we now understand the life-long concern that parents have for children, and no longer feel the intense resentment toward our own parents' anxieties about our welfare. Furthermore, as a parent now of two young adults we realize that our anxieties about their life do not end because they are adults, but continue in different ways. These realizations not only affect our own roles as a son, parent, and mate, but our functioning as a therapist who is seeking to understand others. No matter at what time of life we find ourselves, we are living a variety of roles from which we can learn. And as life evolves, these roles will change and affect the way we view ourselves and others. Perhaps this is the most important lesson of life: that nothing remains the same; nothing lasts forever. In the words of Lucretius:

> No single thing abides, but all things flow.
> Fragment to fragment clings; the things thus grow
> Until we know and name them. By degrees
> They melt, and are no more the things we know.

Chapter 9

SOME AFTERTHOUGHTS

These thoughts constitute a personal journal of our beliefs, prejudices, and ideas that we think particularly worthy of note and remembrance for the practicing psychotherapist.

ACCEPTANCE

Learning to accept another human being is one of the most difficult things that we need to do in our relations with others. Acceptance signifies that we acknowledge and embrace the boundless differences in others without moralizing, judging, and imposing our own ways. It means nothing less than taking people for what they are and not trying to make them over in your image. This problem confronts us daily: learning to accept the compulsive cleanliness of a mate, the way in which teenage offspring wears her hair, the politics of a friend, or the customs of an older generation. When you accept another, you show approval and reveal that you are secure within yourself to embrace diversity. Truly a Herculean task that pervades our human existence, acceptance is the foundation of love and personal security.

CURE

It is customary for therapists to state that no patient is ever really "cured," but that the patient is just helped to cope better with a problem that will never go away. We disagree with this view which, often, reflects false humility or a rationalization for therapeutic failure. Therapy can cure people of irrational behavior and distorted thinking; to believe and think otherwise is a negative approach to the practice of psychotherapy. We acknowledge, however, that conflicts can persist throughout much of an individual's life, as for example, the hatred of a parent and its repercussions in love relationships. Still, therapy can help the individual to minimize and combat the self-destructive ways of dealing with such profound human conflicts. Our emphasis is for a positive and optimistic therapeutic approach, yet cognizant that a successfully treated problem can erupt, under a specific set of pressures and crises, and return to disorganize the individual. We also recognize that in severe personality disturbances like psychosis, psychotherapeutic intervention may be of limited value. Nevertheless, the psychotherapist should be ever cautious that therapeutic failures and limitations do not undermine the positive and confident outlook that should pervade therapeutic endeavors.

EMERGENCIES

Helping emotionally disturbed people requires that the therapist be available in times of crisis. A patient under severe stress cannot always wait for the next therapy session to discuss an urgent problem. Therefore, let the patient know when and where you can be reached; your telephone number will suffice. The patient must be reassured that his cry for help in an emergency will be responded to. If you question the nature of the patient's "emergency," then discuss these doubts with the patient. Emphasize your availability but stress that anxieties aroused in the course of therapy are natural and should be discussed in the next session and not in an emergency call. Always show your concern and support to the patient within a firm therapeutic structure. Unfortunately, some therapists, especially those who are inexperienced, view such calls as an invasion of their privacy or as a form of manipulation. Consequently, these therapists will not respond to such calls, and even warn the patient against contact other than during the regular therapy session. We deplore this attitude and view it not only as insensitivity, but as professional irresponsibility. As stated earlier, in over 30 years of practice, we have found only a few patients who have abused this offer of availability. This is part of the hazard and inconvenience of practicing psychotherapy. If you cannot cope with patient emergencies such as imminent psychotic breaks, suicidal gestures, a divorce threat, a loss of job, a sudden death, then you should reexamine your therapeutic philosophy.

FAILURE

At times, every clinician will experience a patient who cannot be helped for one or more reasons. Although it is admirable to feel that every patient can benefit from therapy, it is most important to recognize and admit failure. Acknowledging failure enables the therapist to understand the limits in himself and in the patient. First, each clinician has personal strengths and weaknesses that become triggered by certain patients. Some therapists work well only with children and teenagers, and have difficulties with adult patients. Others have successes with patients of all ages who are phobic, depressed, and obsessive, and fail with aggressive, antisocial individuals who may also be acting out. Still others cannot work with addictive or alcoholic personalities, but can be effective with borderline and psychotic patients. We urge that every therapist learn his limitations and try to understand why a particular diagnostic category or age group presents problems for you. For example, the newly married therapist may be threatened by and unable to work with patients experiencing marital problems; the young clinician struggling with his own independence may be unable to work with aggressive parental types. As you learn your own limitations, your therapeutic effectiveness will increase. Accordingly, follow your strengths and take on patients who conform to your assets and not your vulnerabilities. Patients with whom you cannot work should be referred to another practitioner or mental health agency.

Second, therapeutic failure can be caused by the patient himself. There are resistant patients who have come to therapy only to please someone else or because they have been forced into it. Other patients are unable to relate and feel uncomfortable in a close interpersonal situation such as therapy, and they are too threatened to ever talk about themselves. Then there are individuals who have lived many years developing habits and a life-style that are resistant to modification. In brief, insurmountable resistances of the patient will lead to therapeutic failure. When this situation occurs, the therapist should terminate therapy if, after a discussion of the patient's resistance, there is no change for the better. Also, the therapist should advise the patient that he may be more ready for therapy at some future time. Always leave or terminate with a patient on a positive note and count on the possibility that this patient may seek help in the future because you accepted his right to resist at this time.

In summary, when therapeutic failure occurs, the therapist should make every attempt to understand the reasons for failure, effect a termination and not perpetuate a stalemate that will only reenforce resistance and mutual resentment. Moreover, the therapist must take the responsibility for helping the patient obtain therapy from someone else, and, failing that, end therapy in a courteous and accepting manner. Most important, failure is a therapeutic reality from which we can all learn.

HAPPINESS

People throughout history have sought the solution to happiness. As if there were a formula that would create happiness, people seek advice and follow special emotional diets to become happy. Witness the purveyors of happiness today with their endless prescriptions and remedies (Brody, 1979). They tell you that happiness is letting it all hang out, overcoming your "erroneous zones," expressing your innermost emotions, being your best friend, looking out for "number one," and taking charge of your life. You can also become happy by meditating, "esting," screaming, encountering, and touching. Given sufficient motivation and interest, any one of these remedies may offer a temporary measure of increased well-being. But with time, like any diet or guaranteed cure, the person will resume his modus operandi. Too often, these magic formulas can backfire by creating unrealistic expectations in persons who would achieve a happier life if they listened to their own needs and emotions. Another difficulty created by much of this advice is that it stresses being dangerously self-centered and narcissistic; it teaches one to ignore the rights and needs of others. Furthermore, the endless how-to- books on achieving happiness present a bewildering array of contradictions that lead to more confusion than understanding.

Psychotherapy cannot offer a "recipe" for happiness. Therapy can, however, help an individual understand that there is no formula for happiness and that the achievement of happiness requires a lifelong search. It also teaches that happiness cannot pervade every moment of our lives and that being unhappy is a natural part of life with which we must learn to accept and cope. Moreover, psychotherapy can lead to the understanding that happiness reflects a highly individual lifestyle which does not have to conform to a specific formula of "shoulds" and "should nots." We believe that people would be happier if they could learn to accept themselves and understand these principles which essentially represent the goals of psychotherapy.

HUMAN NATURE

Human nature, the essence of being, is one of the eternal questions for which man has tried to find an answer. Philosophers, scientists, artists, and the religious throughout the ages have attempted to explain human nature with varying degrees of success. Although the greatest thinkers have provided many profound theories and insights into our behavior, the only fact upon which there seems to be agreement is our basic inability to fully know and explain man's being. Human nature is an eternal mystery, an idea that has profound implications for the psychotherapist.

As therapists, searching together with a patient for explanations and answers to behavior, we must constantly be aware of our limitations in achieving complete understanding of another and even ourselves. Clinicians need to acknowledge that everything is not explainable and our ability to fully understand human nature is limited; a humbling thought, which should always be kept uppermost in our minds to prevent the development of false pride and clinical omniscience. If we cannot know and account for everything, then we can understand that all patients have a right to individual privacy which should not be invaded by the therapist. In a beautiful and profound book on "Man's Unconquerable Mind," the classical scholar, Gilbert Highet, (1954, p. 35) wrote:

> We are not intended to only diagnose and calculate, but also to wonder; to admire; to expect the unexpected.

Human nature is ultimately unknowable and a mystery. The medieval thinkers, as Highet reminds us, summed up our limit to knowledge in one of the truest sayings ever spoken:

Omnia exevnt in mysterivm
All things pass into mystery

Despite man's inability to fully comprehend human nature, there are certain fundamental ideas about human behavior that therapists should never lose sight of. The most important is the powerful influence of the mind. Although scholars still struggle with the mind and body problem, (i.e., whether man is explained in terms of either the mental or the physical, or a combination of both), clinical evidence clearly demonstrates that the concept of mind cannot be ignored or relegated to second-class status. Even if the reader cannot subscribe to our belief that mind and body constantly interact to cause behavior, the therapist must be aware of the importance of the mind's influence. There seems to us no better or dramatic illustration that there is no real separation between mind and body than in the effect of a placebo, an imitation medicine given to placate the patient, that can significantly aid in combating organic illness. Placebo effects demonstrate vividly the powers of suggestion. In three thought-provoking articles, Norman Cousins (May 1977, Oct 1977, 1978) described how he conquered a rare and supposedly incurable illness by "exercising the will to live." Cousins outlined how a self-prescribed diet of laughter (reading humorous literature and watching comedy films), helped maintain a positive attitude and aided in overcoming pain. Every health practitioner should read these articles which illustrate that "The will to live is not a theoretical abstraction, but a physiologic reality with therapeutic characteristics" (May 1977, p. 6).

The psychotherapist can apply this knowledge of the mind's influences in many ways: ascertaining the emotional outlook of the patient or the extent to which the person's reactions reflect a positive attitude in dealing with the world; using the power of suggestion in a judicious and well-timed manner to reenforce a positive outlook; being cognizant that the patient's awe and faith in you as an expert represents an inherent therapeutic advantage which should never be undermined by unethical professional behavior; realizing that bodily complaints may have to some degree a psychosomatic or emotional basis that need to be clarified.

A final idea about human nature is the complex problem of human motivation. No one will ever exhaust the list of motives for human behavior. However, every therapist should develop a basic theoretical framework of causation on which to hang his therapeutic explanations and strategy. Our framework views love (romantic, erotic, familial, social), power (aggression, money, self-enhancement), and the fear of death as comprising the prime movers of behavior. However simplistic it may sound, we urge that the therapist make constant and repeated efforts to understand how these basic human strivings and concerns are thwarted and fulfilled in the patient. Knowing how the patient handles such basic needs is crucial in comprehending his behavior and developing effective therapeutic plans.

INTERMINABLE THERAPY

Over the years of practice every therapist will have a small number of patients who will require an indefinite period of psychotherapy. Such therapy may be continuous or periodically interrupted by long or short absences, depending on the patient's changing life circumstances. It is important to recognize that some situations, however rare, will demand prolonged or indefinite treatment. The therapist must learn to accept this need and avoid viewing it as a therapeutic failure on his part. Our experience indicates that patients who require continuous or intermittent therapy for much of their adult lives are individuals who 1) have actually neither close family nor friends to whom they can turn to for discussion and support, 2) feel estranged from family or friends who are rejecting and emotionally destructive, 3) have some physical affliction or intellectual handicap like a learning disability that causes the person to feel always different and alone, 4) suffer from a chronically weak ego make-up which requires constant bolstering and clarification of reality, and 5) may be borderline psychotic or severely neurotic and require a permanent supportive relationship that consistently defines reality for them.

The single most distinguishing characteristic or common denominator in all these cases is the individual's inability to actually be or feel close to and accepted by another person. These individuals are emotionally isolated from any other human being, and feel all alone in the world. As a result, the therapist becomes the only person to whom they can relate, talk to, and draw emotional sustenance from. What may be so remarkable and paradoxical about such patients is that they may have achieved some degree of vocational success despite this crucial psychological vulnerability and deficiency.

In summary, when patients require indefinite or prolonged treatment, the therapist must 1) not view their need as his therapeutic failure, 2) accept and understand the need for extended therapy, and 3) conduct treatment essentially in a supportive manner. Finally, the therapist should be cognizant that such prolonged treatment may be the major factor in preventing more serious personality deterioration, and helping the individual to get through life.

LANGUAGE AND WRITING

Professor David Wechsler of intelligence testing fame used to admonish doctoral students in clinical psychology to learn to speak and write well. He warned the future clinician that without a good knowledge of language and writing, professional proficiency would be sorely limited. Our clinical experience has borne out this wise advice which we presume to pass along. One of the psychotherapist's major tools is language; the ability to express thoughts in a fluent and concise manner and to grasp another's speech in all its nuance. It behooves the therapist to always broaden, improve, and polish vocabulary skills and verbal facility. Moreover, it is imperative that you recognize linguistic differences in patients as everyone's background differs in educational, geographic, cultural, and ethnic influences. A therapist must learn to understand and communicate with patients who display a variety of speech patterns. Thus, your speech may not be the same as the patient who is a Southern college professor, an Italian immigrant carpenter, a New York City high school drop-out, a suburban policeman, or a saleswoman reared in a rural setting.

Despite the linguistic differences in all of us, the therapist's meaning should remain clear and understandable. Do not be afraid to ask the patient to explain himself if you have the slightest doubt about his meaning. Also learn to explain your meaning in various ways if the patient shows any confusion about the sense of your remarks. Misunderstandings represent the greatest problem in communication. Constant efforts must be made by the therapist to be sure the message is clear. Our experience shows that the use of analogies offers the surest and quickest road to comprehension. For example, in helping a rigid and repressed patient understand personality functioning and the potential for growth, we use the analogy of a piano keyboard: a personality is like a keyboard that has the potential for much richness and expression if played effectively: the more you use the entire keyboard, the more satisfying and richer the music. Similarly, the more you use and express yourself, the greater the self-fulfillment; the more inhibited you are, like a piano that plays only within a narrow range of notes, the more unfulfilled and ineffective you will be. Effectiveness in communicating will be greatly increased by developing the use of analogies, metaphors and similies. The challenge and thrill of imparting your observations and insights to the patient is in finding the right words and connotations that will be easily and clearly understood. You can best meet this challenge by assiduously cultivating your own repertoire of analogies and verbal examples.

Writing well is as important for the clinicial as for any other professional. Therapists are constantly asked for written reports about a patient's diagnosis, therapeutic progress, and recommendations. Schools, various mental health agencies, other practitioners, courts, and hospitals represent the major sources from which reports are requested. The therapist's written report can have important consequences for the patient and requires the utmost in clarity, conciseness, and precision. Learning to write is a skill that needs practice and hard work. The most common and loudest complaint of today's educators and employers is the prevalence of poor writing, the inability of people to express themselves in written form. Unfortunately, our own experience confirms this indictment when we read most professional reports. Too many clinical reports are examples of poor writing: bad grammar, fuzzy meanings, run-on sentences, poor punctuation, and, most striking, a combination of jargon and wordiness. In addition, clinical reports often show a lack of structure or format that add to a sloppy written presentation. A corollary of this complaint is the regrettable tendency to avoid keeping adequate notes of therapeutic plans, progress, and terminations.

Writing is another form of communication, a skill that requires knowledge, practice, and attention. It is a slow, laborious process. Putting our thoughts on paper forces us to think. Good writing will reflect clear and precise thinking. We urge every therapist to develop his writing skill; it will clarify thoughts and develop better powers of analysis. Learn to write effectively by using reference tools that should minimally include a comprehensive dictionary, a thesaurus, and books on usage. The book we most value and recommend to everyone interested in improving his writing skill is Strunk and White's *The Elements of Style* (1979, p. 23). In this slim volume of invaluable advice and guides to good writing, Strunk exhorts us again and again to develop clarity, clarity, clarity!

> Vigorous writing is concise. A sentence should contain no unnecessary words, a paragraph no unnecessary sentences, for the same reason that a drawing should have no unnecessary lines and a machine no unnecessary parts. This requires not that the writer make all sentences short, or that he avoid all detail and treat his subjects in outline, but that every word tell.

This emphasis on conciseness and clarity should be the clinician's motto. Above all, the therapist should use words, whether written or spoken, that avoid professional jargon and reflect the simple, direct, and vivid characteristics of everyday language.

Listening

A startling but not uncommon experience is when a stranger suddenly begins to talk about the most intimate and personal details of his life. It illustrates, in part, the enormous need people have to be listened to, to have someone to whom they can talk. In our highly educated and articulate society, everyone talks endlessly, but few really listen. Everyone seems more preoccupied with his own thoughts and reactions than with what another is saying. Our anxiety to impress and show-off our own prowess prevents us from truly listening. Witness the television interview shows where all compete to talk and wait with impatience and self-preoccupation until another has finished speaking. This illustration can be duplicated in practically any situation that finds two or more people engaged in conversation: a family meal, a faculty meeting, a gathering of friends, or any conversation between people.

More than most, the practicing psychotherapist must be mindful of people's insatiable need to ventilate feelings and be listened to. Thousands of years ago Aristotle, in writing about the effects of theater and drama, stressed the importance of catharsis, the opportunity to purge the emotions through artistic expression. Today, catharsis is an established principle of psychotherapy whose importance should never be overlooked or underestimated. Learn to develop the art of listening by establishing an atmosphere that encourages patients to express their thoughts and emotions. This can be accomplished by imparting an attitude of patience, showing a genuine interest in the person's remarks, displaying appropriate silences, and asking questions that elicit and promote talking. When therapists have difficulty in listening, it is because they are preoccupied with impressing patients with their expertise. Beginning therapists usually have problems in listening because they are plagued with anxieties about their inexperience and effectiveness. Consequently, they become concerned with their own reactions rather than the patient's comments. Therapists must also learn to listen with "the third ear,"as Theodore Reik (1956) emphasized. Not only should the therapist try to understand the meaning of a patient's remarks, but he should be aware of implied meanings, or what lies below the surface of a patient's comments. Cultivate this art of being sensitive to the hidden meanings that the patient verbally conceals.

LOVE

The greatest of all human needs is love. If there is any answer to human existence, to man's loneliness and separateness, it is love. Whether romantic, erotic, familial or religious, the basis of love is giving of ourselves. To love others, one must first be able to love oneself. In one of the most comprehensive and profound enquiries into the nature of love, Erich Fromm (1956, p. 59) stresses that "love for and understanding of one's self cannot be separated from respect and love and understanding for another individual. The love for my own self is inseparably connected with the love for any other human being." The implication of this premise for the therapist is to recognize the importance of aiding people in discovering their own worth and developing self-respect. In this age of doing your own thing, narcissism and narcissistic personality disorders are widespread. Narcissism is not self-love, but a manifestation of selfishness; the antithesis of love. Narcissistic people dislike themselves, and are incapable of loving themselves and others. Therapists can help people love only by helping them first to understand that love begins within each of us.

Another characteristic of love which therapists must remember, is that love is an art and skill which needs to be taught and requires practice. (Fromm devotes an entire chapter to the practice of love.) People are not born with an innate knowledge and skill of loving. The art of loving must be learned and practiced. Those who have been fortunate enough to have had loving families and friends during childhood, have a head start on developing a loving skill. However, learning to love also means disciplining ourselves to show care for others. Most of the patients seen by therapists have had little or no experience with love. Therefore, the patient should be helped to understand that love exists in the world. Furthermore, showing the care, concern, respect, and responsibility which characterizes a loving person requires self-discipline and conscious effort.

RELIGION AND PSYCHOTHERAPY

Practicing psychotherapy is the closest thing to practicing a secular religion. Both aim to help individuals achieve a sense of purpose, happiness, peace of mind, and the "good life." Both recognize that "man is a synthesis of the infinite and the finite, of the temporal and the eternal, of freedom and necessity" (Kierkegaard, 1954, p. 146). Both stress love, acceptance, sharing responsibility and self-knowledge in the pursuit of truth and meaning. The importance of this for the therapist is the realization that psychotherapy, like religion, teaches explicitly and implicitly a moral philosophy. Although the therapist must at all costs avoid being judgmental or viewing behavior as either "good" or "bad," every therapist must evaluate the effectiveness of the patient's personal behavior. This evaluation represents a subtle or implicit moral judgment since it must be made according to some set of individual and cultural standards by the therapist. What must be acknowledged is that each therapist's attitude and reactions reflect certain moral beliefs that are directly or indirectly conveyed to the patient. Therefore, every effort must be made by the therapist to accept and understand this reality, and to be continually on guard against imposing his moral values and philosophy of life onto the patient.

In an important and unique text on the morals of psychotherapy, London (1964) describes the therapist as a "moral agent." Even though the therapist is vividly aware of his personal values, and maintains a moral neutrality (which in itself is a moral position), London wisely underscores the insoluble nature of this moral dilemma. Moreover, the lack of attention given by professional training to the moral beliefs and philosophies of people reflects how little preparation most therapists have to deal with this crucial issue. Nevertheless, if psychotherapists

> affirm some technical expertise and wish to claim geniune ability to influence people, then we must assume some responsibility to the nature of that influence. In that event, they must ultimately see themselves as moral agents as they are confronted with moral problems. And the extent to which they are confronted by moral problems depends on the significance of the problems with which they deal, for morals are the ultimate values we assign to our acts.
>
> It is not clear that psychotherapists are suited to assume this role, but it seems certain they cannot escape it. (London, 1964, p. 15)

These thoughts demonstrate that psychotherapy and religion are neither mutually exclusive nor at cross pruposes. Essentially, each seeks to provide meaning or a guidepost to life.

Individuals without a sense of meaning or purpose to their lives will live a drifting, aimless, and frustrated existence. Empirical evidence indicates that the healthy mature person is the one whose life is guided by a strong belief in something. It is irrelevant whether that faith and purpose is found in a formal religion, nature, science, a hobby, or a religion of no belief. What is crucial is that the individual has a guiding star by which he steers his life. It is our feeling that therapy must help each individual to discover for himself the many roads and opportunities to a belief that enriches and enlarges his daily existence.

TECHNIQUE

Every practitioner continually strives to develop new therapeutic techniques and perfect old ones. Training, supervision, and experience aim at maximizing the therapist's effectiveness. In our technological society, the emphasis is on becoming a first-class technician. Any technician possesses highly trained skills that are applied in an objective, impersonal, mechanistic, and perfectionistic fashion. Psychotherapeutic technique, however, must be more than just the application of a repertoire of perfected skills since the healing process deals with a subject matter that is imperfect and inexact—the nature of man. Therefore, therapy cannot be an exact science like physics or chemistry that requires a strict, objective approach to a clearly defined and impersonal subject. We believe that there are no truly exact or pure sciences but only sciences whose exactness varies according to the degree of subjective involvement required. In the social sciences, the scientist usually becomes personally involved, and uses the interpersonal relationship when studying and dealing with the topic of inquiry. Similarly, psychotherapy requires an intimate and sharing relationship between patient and therapist. Most important, this emotional relationship has a crucial effect on the therapeutic outcome; the quality of the patient–therapist interaction deeply influences the healing process. Consequently, the techniques of psychotherapy must recognize and incorporate something more than just technical skills.

Each therapist must go beyond and transcend technical skills, per se, and recognize the human element that pervades the treatment process. Therapeutic technique should consist not only of well-trained skills, but should, above all, include the ability to reach out emotionally to the troubled person. The therapist must use his emotional being to touch the heart of the patient. All the technique in the world will be rendered ineffective if the therapist is unable to strike a responsive emotional chord in the patient. If the patient does not feel your acceptance, caring, and understanding, no amount of technique will make up for this emotional emptiness. Just as there are gifted artists who leave us cold by their sterile performance, so there are therapists who are quite skilled but leave the patient untouched emotionally. This idea was beautifully expressed centuries ago when Carl Phillip Emmanuel Bach wrote on the art of playing keyboard instruments:

> Keyboard players whose main asset is mere technique clearly are at a disadvantage . . . More often than not, one meets technicians, agile players by profession, who astound us by their prowess without ever touching our feelings . . . A mere technique cannot claim the rewards of those who gently move the heart rather than the ear.

WILL

Therapeutic progress always depends on the patient's will or capacity to act toward a desired goal. We do not refer to the Victorian concept of "will power" which admonishes people to be better, and caused the idea of will to be dismissed by most clinicians. Recently, the importance of will is being rediscovered as evidenced in books by Arieti (1972) and May (1969). Our view is that will arises from understanding or insight. As

William James (1950) explained in his famous *Principles of Psychology*, will and belief are inseparably connected: the "healthy will" is defined as action following belief. The therapist's ultimate task is to stimulate the patient's will by providing the patient with understanding and liberating him from the "thou shalls" and "thou shall nots" that have immobilized his will. A striking example of a complete loss of the ability to will is the catatonic as described by Arieti. Creating awareness in the patient, showing the self-destructive effects of fear, repression, and moralizing will lead to action. Or, as Rollo May's concept of "intentionality" indicates: the meaning of each experience implies a committment, an intention.

One of the most difficult and complex challenges faced by each therapist is the problem of will. How do you get the patient to act constructively and positively in his own behalf? How do you get the patient to act on the ideas he knows will lead to self-fulfillment and liberation from harmful psychic forces? It will not happen by exhortation, admonishment, or advice, but by helping the patient achieve understanding and awareness that lead to freedom from irrational and inhibiting thoughts and feelings. Moreover, we would encourage each therapist to explain the concept of will and its importance in achieving therapeutic progress. Such an explanation is not quiet persuasion, but reflects the therapist's own obligation to impart awareness and understanding. All of us need to understand that health, happiness, and success are not innately given, but require hard work and constant effort to attain.

WORK AND PLAY

The work of a psychotherapist is hard and wearing, but exhilarating and challenging. It requires infinite patience, compassion, and empathy. Probably, its most demanding aspect is the high degree of concentration and awareness it necessitates. The therapist's attention must always be focused on the patient;

the slightest inattention can cause problems in relating and understanding. Every therapy session should ideally have you working at the top of your form, and giving your all to the patient. It is like being on center stage every moment. These exacting expectations can easily create mental fatigue, tension, and stress in any therapist.

Therapists must be aware of these built-in psychic hazards, and constantly guard against them. The best remedy to combat the effects of this highly-charged emotional atmosphere of therapy is to develop a well-rounded life of work and play. Sufficient recreation and other interests should balance your intensely lived life as a therapist. Getting away from your practice by taking vacations and pursuing other interests insures the relaxation that enables you to maintain a fresh approach to therapy. This need probably explains why so many therapists wisely take the entire summer as vacation time and generated Woody Allen's complaint that when you need a shrink in the summer, you cannot get one in Manhattan because they are all away on vacation. Travel, sports, art, theater, opera, travel, reading, playing music, anything that gives you a chance to be away and to be with people other than patients is hereby prescribed as mandatory. Without opportunities to relax, the therapist's best instrument, himself, will become overworked and deteriorate.

There are other psychic hazards which create stress in the therapist besides the emotionally intense atmosphere of therapy session (Chessick 1978). First, listening and being exposed daily to human suffering and tragedy can become an oppressive experience. Moreover, constant exposure to human unhappiness and anguish can be contagious. The therapist may dwell upon the anguish of others and allow it to infect him. A second hazard is the unresolved personal problems that exist in the therapist. Some practitioners are drawn to the profession in hope of healing their own conflicts, a situation that makes them vulnerable to the plight of disturbed patients. Last, the lonely setting of therapy can generate a sense of isolation that can turn the therapist excessively inward. In describing the "sad soul" and the "anguish" of therapists, Chessick (1978) prescribed many remedies: contact with "healthy souls"; awareness; developing a firm sense of self and a capacity to love; and seeking psychotherapy. To this list we would add the importance of recreation or the pursuit of outside interests.

WONDERS

When we review man's development and history, one trait stands out boldly from all others: the will to survive. Time and again man overcomes whatever tragedy or catastrophe befalls him. Since civilization began individuals have shown an awesome, incredible, and boundless resiliency to rise from the ashes and begin again. Examples are everywhere: the survivors of the Nazi concentration camps who forged the new nation of Israel; the European countries that were physically and morally destroyed during World War II which are now brimming with vitality; the victims of Hiroshima who have rebuilt their lives, city, and country; and the Greek, Roman, and Asian civilizations that disintegrated and rose again. Just as nations and civilizations have conquered adversity, the individual has also perservered to triumph over personal misfortune: the handicapped Helen Keller, the imprisoned Solzhenitsyn, the poverty stricken Mahatma Ghandi, and the crippled Franklin Delano Roosevelt. The examples of perseverance and personal courage abound. Through suffering, perhaps more than through love, man's indomitable spirit to survive and overcome is best demonstrated. Suffering and personal affliction seem able to set in motion the health and strength in each of us to resist and endure.

From this history of man's unconquerable will to survive, the therapist can draw two invaluable principles. First, a view of life that is essentially positive and optimistic, yet aware of man's inhumanity to man and individual misfortune. No better description of such a realistic outlook is the one made by the eminent scholar René Dubos, (1973, pp. 14–15) who describes himself as a "despairing optimist."

> I learned very early that persons and societies can recover from many ordeals and later become fairly successful. This awareness has helped me to maintain an equilibrium between despair and hope . . . I have an enormous faith in the resiliency of human beings and of natural systems. Indeed, I take great pleasure in watching people and places rebound after a disaster . . . I am impressed in particular by the ability of human beings and of whole civilizations to change the course of their social trends, to start on new ventures, and often to take advantage of apparently hopeless situations for developing entirely novel formulas of life . . . I believe that optimism is essential for action and constitutes the only attitude compatible with sanity. Optimism is a creative philosophical attitude, because it encourages taking advantage of personal and social crises for the development of novel and more sensible ways of life.

While we feel despair at man's afflictions and self-destruction, we can hope for a better future; while we embrace an optimistic view that things will be better, we recognize the human failures that tinge hope with despair. Therapists who can develop and maintain this kind of qualified optimism are in the best position to accept and deal with the unceasing negative and pessimistic reactions of most patients. In response to a patient's pessimism and endless complaints about how bad things are, we regularly use a specific technique. We agree with the patient that people and experiences can be destructive, but we ask the patient to consider the following: if you meet 100 people or have 100 different experiences in the course of a week, you will probably have many bad experiences, perhaps 50 percent or more will be negative or harmful, but 50 percent more or less will be positive and rewarding experiences, therefore, you have the choice to view life negatively or positively, or as a realistic combination of both attributes. The crucial point here is to help the patient realize that life is not just full of despair and doom, but that life can be good and rewarding.

The second principle that can be drawn from man's will to survive is the recognition of health within each of us. No matter how unhealthy, every human being has the potential for healthy growth; everyone has inner resources of strength and health that may be masked but can be uncovered and mobilized. The clinician should not only diagnose the maladjustments but should be aware of the signs of strength within every patient. Each person's desire for health and a better life represents an important asset for the therapist.

The first lesson we ever learned about understanding human behavior was to look for each patient's positive traits among the personality problems and weaknesses. This advice never fails to ring true and repeatedly makes us feel astonishment, admiration, and wonder for every human being. We would choose to end this work with that first sage lesson about human behavior taught to us so many years ago, and rendered in more pithy and beautiful words by Sophocles:

> Wonders are many, but none,
> none is more wondrous than man.

REFERENCES

Allport, G. 1937. *Personality, a psychological interpretation.* New York: Henry Holt.

Angyal, A. 1965. *Neurosis and treatment.* New York: Wiley.

Arieti, S. 1972. *The will to be human.* New York: Quadrangle.

Berne, E. 1966. *Principles of group treatment.* New York: Oxford University Press.

Bloom, F. 1977. Psychotherapy and moral culture: A psychiatrist's field report. *The Yale Review* 321–326.

Brody, J. Can happiness be formulated? New York: *The New York Times,* Jan. 7, 1979, pp. C1 and C7.

Camus, A. 1969. *Notebooks 1935–1942.* New York: Harvest/HBJ.

Chessick, R. D. 1969. *How psychotherapy heals.* New York: Science House.

Chessick, R. D. 1978. The sad soul of the psychiatrist. *Bulletin of the Menninger Clinic* 42:1–9.

Cousins, N. Anatomy of an illness (as perceived by the patient). *Saturday Review,* May 28, 1977, p. 4–6.

Cousins, N. The mysterious placebo. *Saturday Review,* Oct. 1, 1977, pp. 9–16.

Cousins, N. What I learned from 3,000 doctors. *Saturday Review,* Feb. 18, 1978, pp. 13–16.

Dahlberg, C. C. 1970. Sexual contact between patient and therapist. *Contemporary Psychoanalysis* 6:107–124.

Dubos, R. The despairing optimist. *The American Scholar 43*: Winter, 1973–74, 14–15.

Feifel, H., and Eells, J. 1963. Patients and therapists assess the same psychotherapy. *Journal of Consulting Psychology* 27:310–318.

Frankl, V. E. 1963. *Man's search for meaning.* New York: Washington Square Press.

Freud, S. 1950–1957. *Collected Papers, Vol. I–V, London original printing 1924.* London: The Hogarth Press.

Fromm, E. 1956. *The art of loving.* New York: Harper.

Fromm-Reichmann, F. 1950. *Principles of intensive psychotherapy.* Chicago: University of Chicago Press.

Gendlin, E. T. 1962. *Experiencing and the creation of meaning.* Glencoe: The Free Press of Glencoe.

Goldstein, A. P. 1967. *Therapist-patient expectancies in psychotherapy.* New York: Macmillan.

Greenson, R. R. 1967. *The technique and practice of psychoanalysis,* vol. 1. New York: International Universities Press.

Heinlein, R. A. 1961. *Stranger in a strange land.* New York: Putnam.

Highet, G. 1954. *Man's unconquerable mind.* New York: Columbia University Press.

James, W. 1950. *Principles of psychology.* New York: Dover.

Jung, C. G., von Franz, M. L., Henderson, J. L., Jacobi, J., and Jaffe, A. 1964. *Man and his symbols.* Garden City, N.Y.: Doubleday.

Kierkegaard, S. 1954. *Fear and trembling and sickness unto death.* New Jersey: Princeton University Press.

Kopp, S. B. 1972. *If you meet the Buddha on the road, kill him!* Ben Lomond, Ca.: Science and Behavior Books.

Lazarus, A. A. 1971. *Behavior therapy and beyond.* New York: McGraw-Hill.

London, P. 1964. *The modes and morals of psychotherapy.* New York: Holt.

Loor, M. 1964. Client perceptions of therapists: A study of the therapeutic relation. *Journal of Consulting Psychology* 29:146–149.

McLuhan, M. 1964. *Understanding media.* New York: McGraw-Hill.

May, R. *Love and will.* 1969. New York: Norton.

Menninger, K. A., and Holzman, P. S. 1973. *Theory of psychoanalytic technique,* 2nd ed. New York: Basic Books.

Moos, R. H., and Clemes, S. R. 1967. Multivariate study of the patient-therapist system. *Journal of Consulting Psychology* 31:119–130.

Nelson, M. C., ed. 1968. *Roles and paradigms in psychotherapy.* New York: Grune & Stratton.

Overstreet, H. A. 1949. *The mature mind.* New York: Norton.

Pearce, J. C. 1974. *Exploring the crack in the cosmic egg.* New York: The Julian Press.

Reik, T. 1956. *Listening with the third ear.* New York: Grove Press.

Reusch, J. 1961. *Therapeutic communication.* New York: Norton.

Robbins, L. L., and Herman, M. 1978. Karl Menninger—still ahead of his time. *Bulletin of the Menninger Clinic* 42:291–305.

Rogers, C. R., and Dymond, R. F. 1964. *Psychotherapy and personality change.* Chicago: University of Chicago Press.

Rubin, T. I. 1975. *Compassion and self-hate.* New York: McKay.

Siegel, M. 1977. Commentary on confidentiality. *American Psychological Association Monitor* 8.

Stollak, G. E., Guerney, B. G., and Rothberg, M., eds. 1966. *Psychotherapy research—Selected readings.* Chicago: Rand McNally.

Strunk, W. Jr., and White, E. B. 1979. *The elements of style.* 3d ed. New York: Macmillan.

Strupp, H. H. 1969. *Patients view their psychotherapy.* Baltimore: Carlton Press.

Strupp, H. H. 1975. On failing one's patient. *Psychotherapy* 12:39–41.

Sullivan, H. S. 1954. *The psychiatric interview.* New York: Norton.

Truax, C. B. 1963. Effective ingredients in psychotherapy: An approach to unraveling the patient-therapist interaction. *Journal of Counseling Psychology* 10:256–263.

Tyler, F. B., and Simmons, W. L. 1964. Patient's conceptions of therapists. *Journal of Clinical Psychology* 20:122–133.

Van Emde, B. C. 1966. Some reflections on sexual relations between physicians and patients. *Journal of Sex Research* 2:215–218.

Webster's New Collegiate Dictionary. Springfield, Mass: Merriam.

INDEX